3
Hi

D0914029

DISCARD

Bloom's Modern Critical Interpretations

The Adventures of
   Huckleberry Finn
Alice's Adventures in
   Wonderland
All Quiet on the
   Western Front
As You Like It
The Ballad of the Sad
   Café
Beloved
Beowulf
Billy Budd, Benito
   Cereno, Bartleby the
   Scrivener, and Other
   Tales
Black Boy
The Bluest Eye
Cat on a Hot Tin
   Roof
The Catcher in the
   Rye
Catch-22
The Color Purple
Crime and
   Punishment
The Crucible
Darkness at Noon
Death of a Salesman
The Death of Artemio
   Cruz
The Divine Comedy
Don Quixote
Dubliners
Emerson's Essays
Emma
Fahrenheit 451
Frankenstein

The Grapes of Wrath
Great Expectations
The Great Gatsby
Hamlet
The Handmaid's Tale
Heart of Darkness
I Know Why the
   Caged Bird Sings
The Iliad
Jane Eyre
The Joy Luck Club
The Jungle
Long Day's Journey
   Into Night
Lord of the Flies
The Lord of the Rings
Love in the Time of
   Cholera
Macbeth
The Man Without
   Qualities
The Metamorphosis
Miss Lonelyhearts
Moby-Dick
Night
1984
The Odyssey
Oedipus Rex
The Old Man and the
   Sea
On the Road
One Flew Over the
   Cuckoo's Nest
One Hundred Years of
   Solitude
The Pardoner's Tale
Persuasion

Portnoy's Complaint
A Portrait of the
   Artist as a Young
   Man
Pride and Prejudice
Ragtime
The Red Badge of
   Courage
The Rime of the
   Ancient Mariner
The Rubáiyát of
   Omar Khayyám
The Scarlet Letter
A Separate Peace
Silas Marner
Song of Solomon
The Stranger
A Streetcar Named
   Desire
Sula
The Sun Also Rises
The Tale of Genji
A Tale of Two Cities
The Tempest
Their Eyes Were
   Watching God
Things Fall Apart
To Kill a Mockingbird
Ulysses
Waiting for Godot
The Waste Land
White Noise
Wuthering Heights
Young Goodman
   Brown

Bloom's Modern Critical Interpretations

Samuel Beckett's
Waiting for Godot
New Edition

Edited and with an introduction by
Harold Bloom
Sterling Professor of the Humanities
Yale University

BLOOM'S
LITERARY CRITICISM
An imprint of Infobase Publishing

Bloom's Modern Critical Interpretations: Waiting for Godot—New Edition

Copyright © 2008 Infobase Publishing

Introduction © 2008 by Harold Bloom

Bloom's Literary Criticism
An imprint of Infobase Publishing
132 West 31st Street
New York NY 10001

Library of Congress Cataloging-in-Publication Data
Samuel Beckett's Waiting for Godot / [edited and with an introduction by] Harold Bloom. — New ed.
     p. cm. — (Bloom's modern critical interpretations)
  Includes bibliographical references and index.
  ISBN 978-0-7910-9793-9 (sh)
 1. Beckett, Samuel, 1906–1989. En attendant Godot. I. Bloom, Harold.
 II. Title: Waiting for Godot.

  PQ2603.E378E677 2008
  842'.914—dc22
                                2007049864

Contributing Editor: Portia Williams Weiskel
Cover designed by Takeshi Takahashi

Printed in the United States of America
Bang EJB 10 9 8 7 6 5 4 3 2 1

This book is printed on acid-free paper.

Contents

Contents

Editor's Note

My Introduction regards *Waiting for Godot* as a Gnostic drama, akin to Shelley's vision. It is no accident that Shelley is so real a presence in Beckett's play. I think that Shelley would have judged Pozzo to be Godot, which is a dreadful thought.

Time, the malign entity for Gnosticism, is analyzed in *Godot* by Richard Schechner, after which Walter D. Asmus gives an account of Beckett as his own director.

Martin Esslin defines theater of the Absurd, while Katherine H. Burkman sees the play's function as initiation, and Normand Berlin tries to define the aesthetic pleasure of *Godot*.

Endgame is compared to *Godot* by Michael Worton, after which Ruby Cohn gives us an informed sketch of the drama.

The problem of what lies beyond *Godot* is taken up by Christopher Devenney, while existentialism is invoked by Lois Gordon.

Gerry Dukes and Rónán McDonald give us contrary visions of *Godot*, both persuasive, again demonstrating that the play's enigmas are insoluble.

HAROLD BLOOM

Introduction

Hugh Kenner wisely observes that, in *Waiting for Godot,* bowler hats "are removed for thinking but replaced for speaking." Such accurate observation is truly Beckettian, even as was Lyndon Johnson's reflection that Gerald Ford was the one person in Washington who could not walk and chew gum at the same time. Beckett's tramps, like President Ford, keep to one activity at a time. Entropy is all around them and within them, since they inhabit, they are, that cosmological emptiness the Gnostics name as the *kenoma*.

Of the name *Godot,* Beckett remarked, "and besides, there is a rue Godot, a cycling racer named Godot, so you see, the possibilities are rather endless." Actually, Beckett seems to have meant Godet, the one-time director of the Tour de France, but even the mistake is Beckettian and reminds us of a grand precursor text, Alfred Jarry's "The Passion Considered as an Uphill Bicycle Race," with its superb start: "Barabbas, slated to race, was scratched."

Nobody is scratched in *Waiting for Godot,* but nobody gets started either. I take it that "Godot" is an emblem for "recognition," and I thereby accept Deirde Bair's tentative suggestion that the play was written while Beckett waited for recognition, for his novels to be received and appreciated, within the canon. A man waiting for recognition is more likely than ever to be obsessed that his feet should hurt continually and perhaps to be provoked also to the memory that his own father invariably wore a bowler hat and a black coat.

A play that moves from "Nothing to be done" (referring to a recalcitrant boot) on to "Yes, let's go," after which they do not move, charmingly does not progress at all. Time, the enemy above all others for the Gnostics, is the adversary in *Waiting for Godot,* as it was in Beckett's *Proust.* That would be a minor truism, if the play were not set in the world made not by Plato's

Demiurge but by the Demiurge of Valentinus, for whom time is hardly the moving image of eternity:

> When the Demiurge further wanted to imitate also the
> boundless, eternal, infinite, and timeless nature of the
> Abyss, but could not express its immutable eternity, being
> as he was a fruit of defect, he embodied their eternity in times,
> epochs, and great numbers of years, under the delusion
> that by the quantity of times he could represent their infinity.
> Thus truth escaped him and he followed the lie.

Blake's way of saying this was to remind us that in equivocal worlds up and down were equivocal. Estragon's way is, "Who am I to tell my private nightmares to if I can't tell them to you?" Lucky's way is the most Gnostic, since how could the *kenoma* be described any better than this?:

> the earth in the great cold the great dark the air and the
> earth abode of stones in the great cold alas alas in the year
> of their Lord six hundred and something the air the earth
> the sea the earth abode of stones in the great deeps the great
> cold on sea on land and in the air I resume for reasons
> unknown in spite of the tennis the facts are there but time
> will tell I resume alas alas on on in short in fine on on
> abode of stones who can doubt it I resume but not so fast
> I resume the skull fading fading fading and concurrently
> simultaneously what is more for reasons unknown.

Description that is also lament—that is the only lyricism possible for the Gnostic, ancient or modern, Valentinus or Schopenhauer, Beckett or Shelley:

>   Art thou pale for weariness
> Of climbing heaven and gazing on the earth,
>   Wandering companionless
> Among the stars that have a different birth—
> And ever changing, like a joyless eye
> That finds no object worth its constancy?

Shelley's fragment carefully assigns the stars to a different birth, shared with our imaginations, a birth that precedes the Creation-Fall that gave us the cosmos of *Waiting for Godot*. When the moon rises, Estragon contemplates it in a Shelleyan mode: "Pale for weariness . . . of climbing heaven and gazing on the likes of us." This negative epiphany, closing act 1, is answered by another extraordinary Shelleyan allusion, soon after the start of act 2:

VLADIMIR: We have that excuse.
ESTRAGON: It's so we don't hear.
VLADIMIR: We have our reasons.
ESTRAGON: All the dead voices.
VLADIMIR: They make a noise like wings.
ESTRAGON: Like leaves.
VLADIMIR: Like sand.
ESTRAGON: Like leaves.
     Silence.
VLADIMIR: They all speak at once.
ESTRAGON: Each one to itself.
     Silence.
VLADIMIR: Rather they whisper.
ESTRAGON: They rustle.
VLADIMIR: They murmur.
ESTRAGON: They rustle.
     Silence.
VLADIMIR: What do they say?
ESTRAGON: They talk about their lives.
VLADIMIR: To have lived is not enough for them.
ESTRAGON: They have to talk about it.
VLADIMIR: To be dead is not enough for them.
ESTRAGON: It is not sufficient.
     Silence.
VLADIMIR: They make a noise like feathers.
ESTRAGON: Like leaves.
VLADIMIR: Like ashes.
ESTRAGON: Like leaves.
     Long silence.
VLADIMIR: Say something!

It is the ultimate, dark transumption of Shelley's fiction of the leaves in the apocalyptic "Ode to the West Wind." Involuntary Gnostics, Estragon and Vladimir are beyond apocalypse, beyond any hope for this world. A tree may bud overnight, but this is not so much like an early miracle (as Kenner says) as it is "another of your nightmares" (as Estagon says). The reentry of the blinded Pozzo, now reduced to crying "Help!" is the drama's most poignant moment, even as its most dreadful negation is shouted by blind Pozzo in his fury, after Vladimir asks a temporal question once too often:

> POZZO: (*suddenly furious*). Have you not done tormenting me with your accursed time! It's abominable! When! When! One day, is that not enough for you, one day he went dumb, one day I went blind, one day we'll go deaf, one day we were born, one day we shall die, the same day, the same second, is that not enough for you? (*Calmer.*) They give birth astride of a grave, the light gleams an instant, then it's night once more.

Pozzo, originally enough of brute to be a Demiurge himself, is now another wanderer in the darkness of the *kenoma*. Estragon's dreadful question, as to whether Pozzo may not have been Godot, is answered negatively by Vladimir, but with something less than perfect confidence. Despite the boy's later testimony, I suspect that the tragicomedy centers precisely there: in the possible identity of Godot and Pozzo, in the unhappy intimation that the Demiurge is not only the god of this world, the spirit of Schopenhauer's Will to Live, but the only god that can be uncovered anywhere, even anywhere out of this world.

RICHARD SCHECHNER

There's Lots of Time in Godot

Two duets and a false solo, that's *Waiting for Godot*. Its structure is more musical than dramatic, more theatrical than literary. The mode is pure performance: song and dance, music-hall routine, games. And the form is a spinning away, a centrifugal wheel in which the center—Time—can barely hold the parts, Gogo and Didi, Pozzo and Lucky, the Boy(s). The characters arrive and depart in pairs, and when they are alone they are afraid: half of them is gone. The Boy isn't really by himself, though one actor plays the role(s). "It wasn't you came yesterday," states Vladimir in Act II. "No Sir," the Boy says. "This is your first time." "Yes Sir." [p. 58b] Only Godot is alone, at the center of the play and all outside it at once. "What does he do, Mr. Godot? ... He does nothing, Sir." [p. 59a] But even Godot is linked to Gogo/Didi. "To Godot? Tied to Godot! What an idea! No question of it. (Pause.) For the moment." [p. 14b] Godot is also linked to the Boy(s), who tend his sheep and goats, who are his messengers. Nor can we forget that Godot cares enough for Gogo/Didi to send someone each night to tell them the appointment will not be kept. What exquisite politeness.

Pozzo (and we must assume, Lucky) has never heard of Godot, although the promised meeting is to take place on his land. Pozzo is insulted that his name means nothing to Gogo/Didi. "We're not from these parts," Estragon says in apology, and Pozzo deigns, "You are human beings none the less."

From *Casebook on Waiting for Godot*, pp. 175–187. © 1967 by Grove Press, Inc.

[p. 15b] Pozzo/Lucky have no appointment to keep. Despite the cracking whip and Pozzo's air of big business on the make, their movements are random, to and fro across the land, burdens in hand, rope in place: there is always time to stop and proclaim. In Act I, after many adieus, Pozzo says, "I don't seem to be able ... (*long hesitation*) ... to depart" And when he does move, he confesses, "I need a running start." In Act II, remembering nothing about "yesterday," Pozzo replies to Vladimir's question, "Where do you go from here," with a simple. "On." It is Pozzo's last word.

The Pozzo/Lucky duet is made of improvised movements and set speeches (Lucky's has run down). The Gogo/Didi duet is made of set movements (they must be at this place each night at dusk to wait for Godot to come or night to fall) and improvised routines spun out of long-ago learned habits. Pozzo who starts in no place is worried only about Time; he ends without time but with a desperate need to move. Gogo-Didi are "tied" to this place and want only for time to pass. Thus, part way through the first act the basic scenic rhythm of *Godot* is established by the strategic arrangement of characters: Gogo/Didi (and later the Boy) have definite appointments, a rendezvous they *must* keep. Pozzo/Lucky are free agents, aimless, not tied to anything but each other. For this reason, Pozzo's watch is very important to him. Having nowhere to go, his only relation to the world is in knowing "the time." The play is a confrontation between the rhythms of place and time. Ultimately they are coordinates of the same function.

Of course, Pozzo's freedom is illusory. He is tied to Lucky—and vice versa—as tightly as the others are tied to Godot and the land. In the scenic calculus of the play, rope = appointment. As one coordinate weakens, the other tightens. Thus, when Pozzo/Lucky lose their sense of time, there is a corresponding increase in their need to cover space. Lucky's speech is imperfect memory, an uncontrollable stream of unconsciousness, while Pozzo's talk is all *tirade*, a series of set speeches, learned long ago, and slowly deserting the master actor, just as the things which define his identity—watch, pipe, atomizer—desert him. I am reminded of Yeats' *Circus Animals' Desertion* where images fail the old poet who is finally forced to "lie down where all the ladders start / In the foul rag-and-bone shop of the heart." Here, too, Pozzo will find himself (Lucky is already there). Thus we see these two in their respective penultimate phases, comforted only by broken bursts of eloquence, laments for that lost love, clock time.

The pairing of characters—those duets—links time and space, presents them as discontinuous coordinates. Gogo/Didi are not sure whether the place in Act II is the same as that in Act I; Pozzo cannot remember yesterday; Gogo/Didi do not recall what they did yesterday. "We should have thought of it [suicide] a million years ago, in the nineties." Gogo either forgets at once, or he never forgets. This peculiar sense of time and place is not centered *in* the characters, but *between* them. Just as it takes two lines to fix a point in space, so it takes two characters to *unfix* our normal expectations of time, place, and being. This pairing is not unique to *Waiting for Godot*; it is a favorite device of contemporary playwrights. The Pupil and the Professor in *The Lesson*, Claire and Solange in *The Maids*, Peter and Jerry in *The Zoo Story*: these are of the same species as *Godot*. What might these duets mean or be? Each of them suggests a precarious existence, of sense of self and self-in-the-world so dependent on "the other" as to be inextricably bound up in the other's physical presence. In these plays "experience" is not "had" by a single character, but "shared" between them. It is not a question of fulfillment—of why Romeo wants Juliet—but of existence. By casting the characters homosexually, the author removes the "romantic" element: these couples are not joined because of some biological urge but because of some metaphysical necessity. The drama that emerges from such pairing is intense and locked-in—a drama whose focus is internal without being "psychological." Internalization without psychology is naked drama, theater unmediated by character. That is why, in these plays, the generic structure of their elements—farce, melodrama, vaudeville—is so unmistakably clear. There is no way (or need) to hide structure: that's all there is. But still, in *Godot*, there are meaningful differences between Vladimir and Estragon, Pozzo and Lucky; but even these shadings of individuation are seen only through the couple: to know one character, you have to know both.

In Aristotelian terms drama is made of the linked chain: action > plot > character > thought. Connections run efficiently in either direction, although for the most part one seeks the heart of a play in its action (as Fergusson uses that term). These same elements are in *Godot*, but the links are broken. The discontinuity of time is reflected on this more abstract level of structure. Thus what Gogo and Didi do is not what they are thinking; nor can we understand their characters by adding and relating events to thoughts. And the action of the play—waiting—is not what they are after but what they want most to avoid. What, after all, are their games for? They wish to "fill time" in such a way that the vessel "containing" their activities is unnoticed amid the activities themselves. Whenever there is nothing "to do" they remember why they are here: To wait for Godot. That memory, that direct confrontation with Time, is painful. They play, invent, move, sing to avoid the sense of waiting. Their activities are therefore keeping them from a consciousness of the action of the play. Although there is a real change in Vladimir's understanding of his experience (he learns precisely what "nothing to be done" means) and in Pozzo's life, these changes and insights do not emerge from the plot (as Lear's "wheel of fire" does), but stand outside of what's happened. Vladimir has his epiphany while Estragon sleeps—in a real way his perception is a function of the sleeping Gogo. Pozzo's understanding, like the man himself, is blind. Structurally as well as thematically, Godot is an "incompleted" play; and its openness is not at the end (as *The Lesson* is open-ended) but in many places throughout: it is a play of gaps and pauses, of broken-off dialogue, of speech and action turning into time-avoiding games and routines. Unlike Beckett's perfectly modulated Molloy, *Waiting for Godot* is designed off-balance. It is the very opposite of *Oedipus*. In *Godot* we do not have the meshed ironies of experience, but that special anxiety associated with question marks preceded and followed by nothing.

What then holds Godot together? Time, habit, memory, and games form the texture of the play and provide both its literary and theatrical interest. In *Proust*, Beckett speaks of habit and memory in a way that helps us understand Godot:

> The laws of memory are subject to the more general laws of habit. Habit is a compromise effected between the individual and his environment, or between the individual and his own organic eccentricities, the guarantee of a dull inviolability, the lightning-conductor of his existence. Habit is the ballast that chains the dog to his vomit. . . . Life is a succession of habits, since the individual is a succession of individuals. . . . The creation of the world did not take place once and for all, but takes place every day.

The other side of "dull inviolability" is "knowing," and it is this that Gogo/Didi must avoid if they are to continue. But knowledge is precisely what Didi has near the end of the play. It ruins everything for him:

> Was I sleeping, while the others suffered? Am I sleeping now? To-morrow, when I wake, or think I do, what shall I say of to-day? That with Estragon my friend, at this place, until the fall of night, I waited for Godot? That Pozzo passed, with his carrier, and that he spoke to us? Probably. But in all that what truth will there be? [Looking at Estragon] He'll know nothing. He'll tell me about the blows he received and I'll give him a carrot. [p. 58a]

Then, paraphrasing Pozzo, Didi continues:

> Astride of a grave and a difficult birth. Down in the hole, lingeringly, the grave-digger puts on the forceps. We have time to grow old. The air is full of our cries. (He listens.) But habit is a great deadener. (He looks again at Estragon.) At me too someone is looking, of me too someone is saying. He is sleeping, he knows nothing, let him sleep on. (Pause.) I can't go on! (Pause.) What have I said?

In realizing that he knows nothing, in seeing that habit is the great deadener—in achieving an ironic point of view toward himself, Didi knows everything, and wishes he did not. For him Pozzo's single instant has become "lingeringly." For Pozzo "the same day, the same second" is enough to enfold all human experience; Didi realizes that there is "time to grow old." But habit will rescue him. Having shouted his anger, frustration, helplessness ("I can't go on!"), Didi is no longer certain of what he said. Dull inviolability has been violated, but only for an instant: one instant is enough for insight, and we have a lifetime to forget. The Boy enters. Unlike the first act, Didi asks him no questions. Instead Didi makes statements. "He won't come this evening.... But he'll come to-morrow." For the first time, Didi asks the Boy about Godot. "What does he do, Mr. Godot? ... Has he a beard, Mr. Godot?" The Boy answers: Godot does nothing, the beard is probably white. Didi says—after a silence—"Christ have mercy on us!" But both thieves will not be saved, and now that the game is up, Vladimir seeks to protect himself:

> Tell him ... (he hesitates) ... tell him you saw me and that ... (he hesitates) ... that you saw me ... (With sudden violence.) You're sure you saw me, you won't come and tell me to-morrow that you never saw me! [p. 59a]

The "us" of the first act is the "me" of the second. Habits break, old friends are abandoned, Gogo—for the moment—is cast into the pit. When Gogo awakens, Didi is standing with his head bowed. Didi does not tell his friend of his conversation with the Boy nor of his insight or sadness. Gogo asks, "What's wrong with you," and Didi answers, "Nothing." Didi tells Estragon that they must return the following evening to keep their appointment once again. But for him the routine is meaningless: Godot will not come. There is something more than irony in his reply to Gogo's question, "And if we dropped him?" "He'd punish us," Didi says. But the punishment is already apparent to Didi: the pointless execution of orders, without hope of fulfillment. Never coming; for Didi, Godot has come ... and gone.

But Didi alone sees behind his old habits and even he, in his ironic musing, senses someone else watching him sleep just as he watches Gogo: he learns that all awareness is relative. Pozzo is no relativist, but a strict naturalist. In the first act he describes the setting of the sun with meticulous hand gestures, twice consulting his watch so as to be precise. Pozzo knows his "degrees" and the subtle shadings of time's passing. He also senses that when night comes it "will burst upon us pop! like that! just when we least expect it." And for Pozzo, once it is night there is no more time, for he measures that commodity by the sun. Going blind, Pozzo too has an epiphany—the exact opposite of Didi's:

Have you not done tormenting me with your accursed time! It's
abominable! When! When! One day, is that not enough for you,
one day he went dumb, one day I went blind, one day we'll go
deaf, one day we were born, one day we shall die, the same day,
the same second, is that not enough for you? [p. 57b]

Of the light gleaming an instant astride the grave, Pozzo has only a dim
memory. He has found a new habit to accommodate his new blindness; his
epiphany is false. The experience of the play indeed shows us that there is
plenty of time, too much: waiting means more time than things to fill it.

Pozzo/Lucky play a special role in this passing of time that is *Waiting
for Godot*'s action. Things have changed for them by Act II. Pozzo is blind and
helpless, Lucky is dumb. Their "career" is nearly over. Like more conventional
theatrical characters, they have passed from bad times to worse. The rope,
whip, and valise remain: all else is gone—Lear and the Fool on the heath, that
is what this strange pair suggests to me. But if they are that in *themselves*, they
are something different to Gogo/Didi. In the first act, Gogo/Didi suspect
that Pozzo may be Godot. Discovering that he is not, they are curious about
him and Lucky. They circle around their new acquaintances, listen to Pozzo's
speeches, taunt Lucky, and so on. Partly afraid, somewhat uncertainly, they
integrate Pozzo/Lucky into their world of waiting: they make out of the
visitors a way of passing time. And they exploit the persons of Pozzo/Lucky,
taking food and playing games. (In the Free Southern Theatre production,
Gogo and Didi pickpocket Pozzo, stealing his watch, pipe, and atomizer—no
doubt to hock them for necessary food. This interpretation has advantages: it
grounds the play in an acceptable reality; it establishes a first act relationship
of double exploitation—Pozzo uses them as audience and they use him as
income.) In the second act this exploitation process is even clearer. Pozzo
no longer seeks an audience. Gogo/Didi no longer think that Pozzo may be
Godot (Gogo, briefly, goes through this routine). Gogo/Didi try to detain
Pozzo/Lucky as long as possible. They play rather cruel games with them,
postponing assistance. It would be intolerable to Gogo/Didi for this "diversion"
to pass quickly, just as it is intolerable for an audience to watch it go on so
long. What "should" be a momentary encounter is converted into a prolonged
affair. Vladimir sermonizes on their responsibilities. "It is not every day that
we are needed." The talk continues without action. Then, trying to pull Pozzo
up, Vladimir falls on top of him. Estragon does likewise. Obviously, they can
pull Pozzo up (just as they can get up themselves). But instead they remain
prone. "Won't you play with us?" they seem to be asking. But Pozzo is in no
playing mood. Despite his protests, Gogo/Didi continue their game. It is, as
Gogo says, "child's play." They get up, help Pozzo and Lucky up, and the play
proceeds. When they are gone, Estragon goes to sleep. Vladimir shakes him

awake. "I was lonely." And speaking of Pozzo/Lucky, "That passed the time." For them, perhaps; but for the audience? It is an ironic scene—the entire cast sprawled on the floor, hard to see, not much action. It makes an audience aware that the time is not passing fast enough.

This game with Pozzo/Lucky is one of many. In fact, the gamesmanship of *Waiting for Godot* is extraordinary. Most of the play is taken up by a series of word games, play acting, body games, routines. Each of these units is distinct, usually cued in by memories of *why* Gogo/Didi are where they are. Unable simply to consider the ramifications of "waiting," unfit, that is, for pure speculation (as Lucky was once fit), they fall back onto their games: how many thieves were saved, how many leaves on the tree, calling each other names, how can we hang ourselves, and so on. These games are not thematically meaningless, they feed into the rich image-texture of the play; but they are meaningless in terms of the play's action: they lead nowhere, they contribute to the non-plot. Even when Godot is discussed, the talk quickly becomes routinized. At one time Vladimir spoke to Godot. "What exactly did we ask him for?" Estragon asks. Vladimir replies, "Were you not there?" "I can't have been listening." But it is Gogo who supplies the information that Didi confirms: That their request was "a kind of prayer . . . a vague supplication." And it is both of them, in contrapuntal chorus, who confirm that Godot would have to "think it over . . . in the quiet of his home . . . consult his family . . . his friends . . . his agents . . . his correspondents . . . his books . . . his bank account . . . before taking a decision."

This kind of conversation populates *Godot*. A discussion or argument is transformed into routinized counterpoint. Much has been said about the beauty of Beckett's prose in this play. More needs to be said about its routine qualities. Clichés are converted into game/rituals by dividing the lines between Gogo and Didi, by arbitrarily assigning one phrase to each. Thus we have a sense of their "pairdom," while we are entranced by the rhythm of their language. Beckett's genius in dialogue is his scoring, not his "book." This scoring pertains not only to language but to events as well. Whatever there is to do, is done in duets. By using these, Gogo/Didi are able to convert anxiety into habit. Gogo is more successful at this than Didi. For Gogo things are either forgotten at once or never forgotten. There is no "time-span" for him, only a kaleidoscopic present in which everything that is there is forever in focus. It takes Didi to remind Gogo of Godot, and these reminders always bring Gogo pain, his exasperated "Ah." For Didi the problem is more complex. Gogo says "no use wriggling" to which Didi replies, "the essential doesn't change." These are opposite contentions; that's why they harmonize so well.

A few words about Time. If waiting is the play's action, Time is its subject. Godot is not Time, but he is associated with it—the one who makes but does not keep appointments. (An impish thought occurs: Perhaps Godot passes time with Gogo/Didi just as they pass it with him. Within this scheme, Godot has nothing to do (as the Boy tells Didi in Act II] and uses the *whole play* as a diversion in his day. Thus the "big game" is a strict analogy of the many "small games" that make the play.) The basic rhythm of the play is habit interrupted by memory—memory obliterated by games. Why do Gogo/Didi play? In order to deaden their sense of waiting. Waiting is a "waiting *for*" and it is precisely this that they wish to forget. One may say that "waiting" is the larger context within which "passing time" by playing games is a subsystem, protecting them from the sense that they are waiting. They confront Time (i.e., are conscious of Godot) only when there is a break in the games and they "know" and "feel" that they are waiting.

In conventional drama all details converge on the center of action. We may call this kind of structure centripetal. In *Godot* the action is centrifugal. Gogo/Didi do their best to shield themselves from a direct consciousness that they are at the appointed place at the prescribed time. If the center of the play is Time, dozens of activities and capers fling Gogo/Didi away from this center. But events at the periphery force them back inward: try as they will, they are not able to forget. . . .

. . . Caught on the hub of this wheel, driven by "reminders" toward the center, Gogo/Didi literally have nowhere to go outside of this tight scheme. The scenic counterpart is the time-bracket "dusk–darkness"—that portion of the day when they must be at the appointed place. But even when night falls, and they are free to go, our last glimpse of them in each act is:

ESTRAGON: Well, shall we go?
VLADIMIR: Yes, let's go.
   They do not move.

As if to underline the duet-nature of this ending, Beckett reverses the line assignments in Act II.

What emerges is a strange solitude, again foreshadowed by Beckett in his *Proust*. "The artistic tendency is not expansive but a contraction. And art is the apotheosis of solitude." In spinning out from the center, Gogo/Didi do not go anywhere, "they do not move." Yet their best theatrical moments are all motion, a running helter-skelter, a panic. Only at the end of each act, when it is all over for the day, are they quiet. The unmoved mover is Time, that dead identicality of instant and eternity. Once each for Didi and Pozzo, everything is contracted to that sense of Time where consciousness is possible, but nothing else. To wait and not know *how* to wait is to experience Time. To be freed from waiting (as Gogo/Didi are at the end of each act) is to permit the moon to rise more rapidly than it can (as it does on *Godot's* stage), almost as if nature were illegally celebrating its release from its own clock. Let loose from Time, night comes all of a sudden. After intermission, there is the next day—and tomorrow, another performance.

There are two time rhythms in *Godot,* one of the play and one of the stage. Theatrically, the exit of the Boy and the sudden night are strong cues for the act (and the play) to end. We, the audience, are relieved—it's almost over for us. They, the actors, do not move—even when the Godot-game is over, the theater-game keeps them in their place: tomorrow they must return to enact identical routines. Underlying the play (all of it, not just the final scene of each act) is the theater, and this is exactly what the script insinuates—a nightly appointment performed for people the characters will never meet. *Waiting for Godot* powerfully injects the mechanics of the theater into the mysteries of the play.

WALTER D. ASMUS

Beckett Directs "Godot"

Beckett is coming to Berlin to direct *Waiting for Godot*. He is no stranger at the Schiller Theater: after *Endgame, Krapp's Last Tape*, and *Happy Days*, this is his fourth visit as a director. He also took part in the rehearsals of *Godot* ten years ago, and it was then that he met the actors Bollman, Wigger, and Herm. Bollman and he had also worked together on *Endgame*.

Rehearsal conditions are ideal: from 28 December to 8 March, mornings only, mostly on stage. Everybody taking part in the production brings enormous sympathy and respect toward Beckett—to such an extent that this will be inevitably, though not obtrusively, reflected in the working process. But he is not only respected as an authority, as a competent interpreter of his own script; more than that the working relationship with him is characterized by caution, attention, concessions, and openness—criteria for attitudes to set free his own attitude. On this basis, everybody tries not to disturb, but to strengthen the tacit mutual trust and to do their job with the highest possible degree of understanding and appreciation toward Beckett. As the weeks go by, there is a strong and at the same time a very vivid and dynamic structure to the group, interchangeable relationships evolving. Beckett's immaculate German is characterized by a typical idiomatic exactness that seems to influence the tone of all taking part. The language gains generally a slight overemphasis, expressive of care and consciousness. As a result of this linguistic precision, most

From *On Beckett: Essays and Criticism,* pp. 280–290. © Grove Press, 1986.

misunderstandings are resolved from the beginning. The everyday colloquial tone ensures a strange, unauthoritarian accent, unusual in the theater.

Should misunderstandings still arise, if only through chance mishearings, everybody, even if only taking part indirectly, is willing to help and clear them up. This atmosphere of constant, concerned alertness, and the pleasure in following up processes, in which an individual might not always be directly involved, is a further reference to the "unauthoritarian" working relationship. People who meet and work with Beckett inevitably seem to end up admiring him.

The rehearsals are carried out in a rather conventional way: After a relatively fast read-through of the script, the detailed work follows with increasing intensity. Content is not being discussed, only (if necessary) situations are cleared up, and with that explanations about the characters given. The great precision of the work and the striving to keep the form as tight as possible are fascinating in themselves. So the necessity to investigate the content of the play is being pushed to the background for the time being (which, of course, has also got something to do with Beckett's well-known aversion to "explaining" his play).

Beckett subjects his own script constantly to critical control in the most amazing and sympathetic way. He is also open to suggestions any time, and he even asks for them. He is not at all interested in carrying out a rigid concept but aims for the best possible interpretation of the script.

Should uncertainty occur, he is ready with a new suggestion the next day, always precise and thought through—even if it does not always work immediately. So it happens that before the second full rehearsal, there is a two-page cut to be discussed, because the scenic transformation remained unsatisfactory. The high degree of consciousness and self-control does not strike the actors as making them performing animals—indeed, they consciously accept it, intensify it, and build on it.

Friday 27 December 1974

Technical rehearsal. Matias, Beckett's designer, talks with the technical director about the stage design, on the stage. I am standing with Beckett at the footlights. He takes off his dark glasses and asks me whether we can rehearse today. No, the technical rehearsal will certainly take too long—added to which we have not asked the actors to come in yet. I pass him one of the scripts, which has been typed up and duplicated after his alterations. He seats himself immediately at a table, and is not distracted by the noise of the building gang on the stage. He is comparing the two scripts page by page, following each line with his pen. A picture of isolated relaxation.

As the chief of the costume department comes up to talk to him, he stands up to explain details about the costumes from the designs. Vladimir is going to wear striped trousers, which fit him, with a black jacket, which is too small for him: The jacket belonged originally to Estragon. Estragon, on the other hand, wears black trousers, which fit him, with a striped jacket, which is too big for him: It originally belonged to Vladimir. In this way, the differing physiques of the two actors, Bollman and Wigger, become part of the whole conceptual consideration. Similarly, Lucky's shoes are the same color as Pozzo's hat, his checked waistcoat matches Pozzo's checked trousers, as his gray trousers do Pozzo's gray jacket.

About Estragon and Vladimir, Beckett says: "Estragon is on the ground, he belongs to the stone. Vladimir is light, he is oriented towards the sky. He belongs to the tree." Beckett speaks very little. He asks me when I started working at the theater, and what did I do before that? There are long pauses between fragments of conversation as we watch the carpenters work on the stage.

When I ask him how he would like the first rehearsals to be, he reacts almost excitedly. No, the stage is not going to be free until 2 January. Is the rehearsal stage as large as this one? It is very important, because of the distance between stone and tree. We will have to be able to create at least almost the same distance, and we are using a raked stage, too.

Are we going to start with the first act up to the Pozzo–Lucky scene tomorrow? I ask him. No, he would like to start off with Lucky's monologue.

Estragon and Vladimir are going to join us at noon. In the meantime, the rake has been built. The carpenters are still experimenting with the moon—the same moon as the one used ten years ago when *Godot* was last played at the Schiller-Theater, partly with Beckett's help. Wigger comes and greets Beckett warmly: "I am very much looking forward to the work." Other members of the company are coming to shake his hand and are seemingly pleased to see him again. Beckett returns the cordiality.

Saturday 28 December 1974

10:00 A.M. on the rehearsal stage: The slope is there, the stone is marked by a small wooden box, a blooming apple tree presents itself Chekhov-fashion.

Almost abruptly, Beckett starts to talk about Lucky's monologue. It is not as difficult as it may seem, he says. We are going to divide it into three parts and the second part is going to be divided again into two sections. The first part is about the indifference of heaven, about divine apathy. This part ends with, "but not so fast.-..." The second part starts off with "considering what is more" and is about man, who is shrinking—about man, who is dwindling. Not only the dwindling is important here, but the shrinking, too. These two points represent the two undersections of the second part. The theme of the third part is "the earth abode of stones" and starts with "considering what is more, much more grave." Beckett is very concerned to be exact in his explanations and to repeat certain ideas, underlining them with short gestures while we are looking for them and marking them.

Herm would like to know, how should he deal with the end of the monologue? Beckett explains that the different elements, belonging to the first three sections, are returning here, at the end. He compares these with a cadence in music: "The threads and themes are being gathered together. The monologue's theme is: to shrink on an impossible earth under an indifferent heaven."

Herm starts to read. Beckett stops him, to undertake some alterations in the script. Instead of *von der anthropopopometrischen Akakakakademie*, it should read *von der Akakakakademie der Anthropopopometrie* (as it stands originally in the English version). The alteration is purely for rhythmical reasons. Herm repeats the line several times. Beckett insists on an exact, rhythmical rendering and reads each syllable with him, underlining it with gestures.

Herm carries on reading. Beckett stops him again and starts reading the lines together with the actor: ". . . that man in short, that man in brief in spite of the strides of alimentation and defecation is seen to waste and pine. . . . He stresses the word *Mensch* (man) making the *sch* into a long, hissing sound. "'Dwindle': that is the climax," he says.

In the next section "the earth abode of stones" is the most important, Beckett points out. The earth is good only for stones. Herm: "I looked up the meaning of Apathie, Athambie, Aphasie: *Gleichgültigkeit, Unerschrockenheit,* and *Sprachlosigkeit.*"

Beckett: "Yes, that is right. It concerns a god who turns himself in all directions at the same time. Lucky wants to say 'Quaquaquaquaversalis,' but he can't bring it out. He says instead only 'quaquaquaqua.'"

Herm: "I have looked them up, the names you use. Peterman was a cartographer."

Beckett: "It is all about stones, about the world of stones."

Herm: "Peterman exists."

"I haven't thought of that," says Beckett. "And Steinweg, the name means *nothing.*"

Herm: "Belcher, that one was a navigator. . . ."

Beckett interrupts him, excited and with delight: "No, Belcher, that is the opposite of Fartov, English to fart. And Belcher, to belch." With one blow the mysticism about Beckettian names is destroyed.

Beckett once again returns to the ideas he thinks most important. He scans "to shrink and dwindle," making a prophetic and threatening gesture with his finger. "To shrink and dwindle ..." will cause bewilderment for the public: but at this point everything will be absolutely clear—for Lucky. Lucky's *thinking* isn't as good as it used to be: "He even used to think prettily once," says Pozzo. Herm could play it that way, watching Pozzo from time to time. And the two others, too. He is not talking simply to himself, he is not completely on his own, says Beckett.

Herm: "But he kind of refuses first, he doesn't like the idea of thinking."

Beckett: "He would like to amuse Pozzo. Pozzo would like to get rid of him, but if he finds Lucky touching, he might keep him. Lucky would like to be successful."

Herm: "He gives Estragon once, a long look. What do you mean to say with this long look?"

Beckett: "It's a kind of look you can't explain in a few words. There is a lot in that look. Lucky wants the piece of bone, of course. Estragon, too. That is a confrontation, a meeting of two very poor people."

Herm: "Something like solidarity, is that in it, too?"

Beckett: "Yes, there are so many things in his head. Recognizing the other one's situation, that is very important—but also some pride, that he is free to dispose of the bones, as opposed to Estragon. But Lucky does not forget either. The kick in the shin should be interpreted as Lucky's revenge for the fact that Estragon took the bone."

Beckett Interprets Lines for the Actors

Beckett carries on with his explanation of the play. It should be done very simply, without long passages, to give confusion shape, he says, a shape through repetition, repetition of themes—not only themes in the script, but also themes of the body. When at the beginning Estragon is asleep leaning on the stone, that is a theme that repeats itself a few times. There are fixed points of waiting, in which everything stands completely still, in which silence threatens to swallow everything up. Then the action starts again.

Wigger: "But in spite of everything, it is at odd moments quite a cheerful game."

Beckett: "Yes, of course, but that should be done very accurately.

The splitting up of Vladimir and Estragon is such a point: They are, in fact, inseparable."

Wigger: "Like a rubber band, they come together time after time."

Beckett: "The principle is: They have to come together step by step."

Beckett walks on the stage, his eyes fixed on the ground, and shows the movement as he speaks Estragon's lines: "You had something to say to me? . . . You're angry? . . . Forgive me. . . . Come, Didi. Give me your hand. . . ."

With each sentence, Beckett makes a step toward the imaginary partner. Always a step, then the sentence. Beckett calls this a step-by-step approach, a physical theme, which comes up five, six, or seven times and has got to be done very accurately. This is the balletic side of the story. Lucky falls twice, and this mustn't be done realistically, but very cleanly.

Wigger: "Does that mean that there is no naturalism left whatsoever?"

Beckett demonstrates: He goes down on his knees and, his arms first upward then stretching forward, lets himself slide on the ground.

Wigger: "But how can one prevent the loss of all human consideration, how can one prevent it from becoming sterile?"

Beckett: "It is a game, everything is a game. When all four of them are lying on the ground, that cannot be handled naturalistically. That has got to be done artificially, balletically. Otherwise, everything becomes an imitation, an imitation of reality."

Wigger: "Are you implying a certain dryness?"

Beckett stands up. "It should become clear and transparent, not dry. It is a game in order to survive."

Beckett in Dialogue with Actors

Beckett continues to make associations with the play: He is very concerned to find clues and to share them with the others.

Beckett: "*Relaxation* is a word of Estragon's. It is his dream, to be able to keep calm. Vladimir is more animated. *Jupiter's son* is wrong: Atlas was not Jupiter's, but Japethos' son."

Wigger: "And no one noticed this in all these years!" (Much laughter.)

Beckett does not like to speak generally about the play. We undertake a discussion of the play, dividing it into different parts. In the first act, there are six parts, in the second, five. They are going to be called A1 to A6 and B1 to B5. Everybody makes the divisions in their scripts. The waiting points (which are not necessarily in accordance with the divisions of the script) are also fixed.

Right at the very beginning, there is an alteration. Estragon is sitting on the stone. Vladimir is standing in the shade near the tree, hard to see. Here is the first waiting point. This is quite an important alteration, that both characters are on stage right from the beginning—as also at the beginning of the second act. But the stage direction in script still says, "*Estragon, sitting on a low mound, is trying to take off his boot. . . . Enter Vladimir.*" But now Bollman and Wigger are sitting next to each other, reading the script continuously till the scene between Pozzo and Lucky. After that the blocking starts. Beckett is on the stage and demonstrates each move exactly on cue, while he speaks the lines, which he knows by heart.

Bollman and Wigger repeat the movements and make notes in their scripts. What Beckett described just now as an approach is becoming clear: Vladimir approaches step-by-step from behind the tree, which stands at the back of the stage to the right. Estragon is sitting on the stone in the front to the left. Vladimir is constantly in motion; Estragon sticks to his stone. The reason for dividing the acts is becoming clear: A2 starts when Estragon stands up and gets moving. With an almost frightening concentration and willpower, A1 and A2 are gone over with absolute precision until the scene with Pozzo and Lucky. The uncompromising attitude with which Beckett returned to the script time after time in the earlier conversation is now transformed into practice.

The Regie Book

In a red hardbound volume of checked paper, a book has been created about another book: a metabook. Written in black ink in English in toy pages, there are detailed directions concerning the whole play.

Pages 2 to 53 contain the scenic arrangements. The right-hand page is mostly used for a written description, while the left hand page is used for sketches or is left blank for corrections or additional notes. The divisions follow those of parts A1 to A6 in the first act and parts B1 to B5 in the second. Each move, each section, is provided with the relevant cue of the German script, underlined each time.

The second part of the book is classified by themes: Lucky's movements; Estragon's feet; Estragon's sleep; the whip; Vladimir, Estragon, and the tree; examination of location (with sketches); doubt—confusions; come, let's go; help; what did I just say; heaven; sleep; to remember; step-by-step approach.

Added to each of the thematic cues are the relevant lines or situations or (as in the case of Lucky's monologue) descriptions or explanations concerning meaning. Both parts are diagonally connected too: In the second, thematic part, there are references to where to find the relevant lines of the first part, and vice versa.

Beckett compiled this regie-book before he came to Berlin. It has to be understood as his attempt to give a scenic outline—a structure—to a play that has been regarded as "not visualized." This is surprising: When one reads the script it appears to be a *non plus ultra* of exactness and form.

When Beckett made the attempt—sitting at his desk—to visualize his play, he knew, of course, why he always left the left-hand page in the regie-book blank. The practice on the stage during the rehearsals led—even if only occasionally—to corrections. Without these additions (in red) the regie-book is now no longer complete. The classification by themes reveals the structure of the production: Although under each heading there is an enumeration of all the places where the theme comes, up it cannot be regarded as a mere catalog. For—and this can be followed through in the diagonal connections—in the blocking and in the construction of the dialogues there is a structure of repetitions, variations, similarities, parallels, of echoes and accumulated references, and these are realized in the production as concrete structure and form.

Tuesday 18 January 1975

The actors are on the stage. It is the usual relaxed starting ritual. While they are still chatting, Beckett walks up and down the stage, his eyes fixed on the ground, glancing at them from time to time. He is concentrating entirely on the coming scene. According to an agreement the day before, the rehearsal starts with Estragon's line "Sweet mother earth," where they are all lying on the ground in the second act. The actors take up their positions of their own accord; the transition from joking and chatting to concentrated rehearsal work happens naturally, almost without a break. The subjective, private attitudes of the actors and the play as a subject of work are correlating in such a way that it produces an atmosphere of "relaxed tension," which could also be described as an occupation of pleasure.

Bollman, Wigger, and Raddatz are lying on the ground. Herm is marked by a rolled-out carpet. It is not essential for him to lie there all the time, Beckett has said. The scene begins. Pozzo creeps away; Estragon and Vladimir are calling him. As they get up, there is an interruption. This structure has been fixed for quite a while, but Beckett would like to tighten it once again. The getting up at the beginning should be done in a normal way, but after that the movements should be slowed down. Bollman and Wigger synchronize once again the gestures between themselves. Then they come halfway up with a slight jerk, whereby they support themselves with their hands (they are lying next to each other), each of them in turn getting up first to the side, then to the back, moving up almost in slow motion and turning toward each other. After a short break, there follows a slow, graceful gesture with both arms, and Estragon's line, "Child's play." Vladimir accentuates his "Simple question of will-power" by performing the well-known obscene gesture with his right arm. Beckett calls this process "ballet-like." Through this formal precision is the meaning both canceled and evident at the same time.

Actors Tease Beckett

Before the second run-through, the following occurs. Bollman, pretending to be serious, says to Herm, who is standing at the footlights watching, "Come here at once and lie down. What are you standing around for?"

Wigger (taking the point): "I can't rehearse like that. . . ."
Herm also reacts to the game: "But Mr. Beckett has said—"
Bollman: "Will you come here at once? What are you getting paid for?"

Beckett smiles somewhat insecurely and watches Herm getting into his lying position. Bollman and Wigger are thrashing Herm on the behind with a pretended childish seriousness. Beckett gets the point and laughs at the echoing of a similar situation in the play:

> ESTRAGON: And suppose, we gave him a good beating, the two of us?
> VLADIMIR: You mean, if we fell on him in his sleep?
> ESTRAGON: Yes.
> VLADIMIR: That seems a good idea all right.

What Bollman and Wigger are carrying out privately, they perform in the context of the play, through a whole range of emotions—joyful, childish, naive and sadistic—yet at the same time with a thrilling, funny kind of anticipation.

The getting up is repeated, and then Vladimir's and Estragon's "staggering" is tidied up. On the turn after Pozzo's question "What is it like?" Beckett has some doubts and would like to cut it. He is very much concerned with tightening the action at this point. They try it without the 360-degree turn.

"What do you think?" Beckett asks.

Herm: "I think it is good to have some motion at this point."

I agree too: "I find that Estragon's line 'Some diversion!' comes out much more strongly after the movement." We stick to the turn for the time being.

Starting with "Sweet mother earth," the scene is being played in context until the exit of Pozzo and Lucky. When Estragon and Vladimir—all lying on the ground—shout, "Pozzo," Beckett slips in a small alteration. Instead of speaking all the time toward the back, toward Pozzo, Estragon should say his "We might try him with other names" directly to Vladimir. There is thus a small intimate moment of conspiracy created at this point, which is reminiscent of similar moments throughout the play.

After a short break for cigarettes, we take the whole section from the entrance of Pozzo and Lucky until the end of the play. Beckett is sitting in the auditorium at his desk with his cigarillo, watching anxiously the "conspiracy scene" between Estragon and Vladimir shortly after the start. He throws something in from time to time but without interrupting the action: "Glance toward Pozzo"; "Both on the top of your toes"—reminding them of things agreed beforehand.

The end of the play: Estragon's trousers are duly falling down. There is loud laughter from the auditorium. Beckett laughs too. Bollman's undershirt has been altered. It now reaches to his calves. It is of pink material, which has been added to but not yet sewn on properly. Bollman stands there looking like a rather unhappy old woman.

Beckett is very pleased with Wigger's monologue shortly before the entrance of the boy. Wigger looks very relaxed, very intense, listening inwardly, and makes only very brief glances around him. The key to this point in action is silence. After the break all scenes starting from Pozzo's entrance to the end of the play are rehearsed again. Beckett sits downstairs making notes. Short corrections are made: "The 'walk' of Estragon and Vladimir should be taken through without stopping; the tiger should 'rush' more in Vladimir's description. After 'Who farted?' jump further back. The pulling up of trousers should only be indicated."

Bollman tries. He is holding his trousers at his belly with his right hand, his pink shirt hanging out on the side. He makes a deplorable but touching picture.

Translated by Ria Julian

MARTIN ESSLIN

Introduction:
The Absurdity of the Absurd

O n 19 November 1957, a group of worried actors were preparing to face their audience. The actors were members of the company of the San Francisco Actors' Workshop. The audience consisted of fourteen hundred convicts at the San Quentin penitentiary. No live play had been performed at San Quentin since Sarah Bernhardt appeared there in 1913. Now, forty-four years later, the play that had been chosen, largely because no woman appeared in it, was Samuel Beckett's *Waiting for Godot*.

No wonder the actors and Herbert Blau, the director, were apprehensive. How were they to face one of the toughest audiences in the world with a highly obscure, intellectual play that had produced near riots among a good many highly sophisticated audiences in Western Europe? Herbert Blau decided to prepare the San Quentin audience for what was to come. He stepped on to the stage and addressed the packed, darkened North Dining Hall—a sea of flickering matches that the convicts tossed over their shoulders after lighting their cigarettes. Blau compared the play to a piece of jazz music 'to which one must listen for whatever one may find in it'. In the same way, he hoped, there would be some meaning, some personal significance for each member of the audience in *Waiting for Godot*.

The curtain parted. The play began. And what had bewildered the sophisticated audiences of Paris, London, and New York was immediately

From *Theatre of the Absurd*, pp. 19–28. © Martin Esslin, 1980.

grasped by an audience of convicts. As the writer of 'Memos of a first-nighter' put it in the columns of the prison paper, the *San Quentin News*:

> The trio of muscle-men, biceps overflowing ... parked all 642 lbs on the aisle and waited for the girls and funny stuff. When this didn't appear they audibly fumed and audibly decided to wait until the house lights dimmed before escaping. They made one error. They listened and looked two minutes too long—and stayed. Left at the end. All shook ...[1]

Or as the writer of the lead story of the same paper reported, under the headline, 'San Francisco Group Leaves S.Q. Audience Waiting for Godot':

> From the moment Robin Wagner's thoughtful and limbo-like set was dressed with light, until the last futile and expectant handclasp was hesitantly activated between the two searching vagrants, the San Francisco company had its audience of captives in its collective hand.... Those that had felt a less controversial vehicle should be attempted as a first play here had their fears allayed a short five minutes after the Samuel Beckett piece began to unfold .[2]

A reporter from the San Francisco *Chronicle* who was present noted that the convicts did not find it difficult to understand the play. One prisoner told him, 'Godot is society.' Said another: 'He's the outside.'[3] A teacher at the prison was quoted as saying, 'They know what is meant by waiting ... and they knew if Godot finally came, he would only be a disappointment.'[4] The leading article of the prison paper showed how clearly the writers had understood the meaning of the play:

> It was an expression, symbolic in order to avoid all personal error, by an author who expected each member of his audience to draw his own conclusions, make his own errors. It asked nothing in point, it forced no dramatized moral on the viewer, it held out no specific hope.... We're still waiting for Godot, and shall continue to wait. When the scenery gets too drab and the action too slow, we'll call each other names and swear to part forever—but then, there's no place to go![5]

It is said that Godot himself, as well as turns of phrase and characters from the play, has since become a permanent part of the private language, the institutional mythology of San Quentin.

Why did a play of the supposedly esoteric avant-garde make so immediate and so deep an impact on an audience of convicts? Because it confronted them with a situation in some ways analogous to their own? Perhaps. Or perhaps because they were unsophisticated enough to come to the theatre without any preconceived notions and ready-made expectations, so that they avoided the mistake that trapped so many established critics who condemned the play for its lack of plot, development, characterization, suspense, or plain common sense. Certainly the prisoners of San Quentin could not be suspected of the sin of intellectual snobbery, for which a sizeable proportion of the audiences of *Waiting for Godot* have often been reproached; of pretending to like a play they did not even begin to understand, just to appear in the know.

The reception of *Waiting for Godot* at San Quentin, and the wide acclaim given to plays by Ionesco, Adamov, Pinter, and others, testify that these plays, which are so often superciliously dismissed as nonsense or mystification, *have* something to say and *can* be understood. Most of the incomprehension with which plays of this type are still being received by critics and theatrical reviewers, most of the bewilderment they have caused and to which they still give rise, come from the fact that they are part of a new and still developing stage convention that has not yet been generally understood and has hardly ever been defined. Inevitably, plays written in thus new convention will, when judged by the standards and criteria of another, be regarded as impertinent and outrageous impostures. If a good play must have a cleverly constructed story, these have no story or plot to speak of; if a good play is judged by subtlety of characterization and motivation, these are often without recognizable characters and present the audience with almost mechanical puppets; if a good play has to have a fully explained theme, which is neatly exposed and finally solved, these often have neither a beginning nor an end; if a good play is to hold the mirror up to nature and portray the manners and mannerisms of the age in finely observed sketches, these seem often to be reflections of dreams and nightmares; if a good play relies on witty repartee and pointed dialogue, these often consist of incoherent babblings.

But the plays we are concerned with here pursue ends quite different from those of the conventional play and therefore use quite different methods. They can be judged only by the standards of the Theatre of the Absurd, which it is the purpose of this book to define and clarify.

It must be stressed, however, that the dramatists whose work is here discussed do not form part of any self-proclaimed or self-conscious school or movement. On the contrary, each of the writers in question is an individual who regards himself as a lone outsider, cut off and isolated in his private world. Each has his own personal approach to both subject-matter and form; his own roots, sources, and background. If they also, very clearly and in spite

of themselves, have a good deal in common, it is because their work most
sensitively mirrors and reflects the preoccupations and anxieties, the emotions
and thinking of many of their contemporaries in the Western world.

This is not to say that their works are representative of mass attitudes.
It is an oversimplification to assume that any age presents a homogeneous
pattern. Ours being, more than most others, an age of transition, it displays
a bewilderingly stratified picture: medieval beliefs still held and overlaid
by eighteenth-century rationalism and mid-nineteenth-century Marxism,
rocked by sudden volcanic eruptions of prehistoric fanaticisms and primitive
tribal cults. Each of these components of the cultural pattern of the age finds
its own artistic expression. The Theatre of the Absurd, however, can be seen as
the reflection of what seems to be the attitude most genuinely representative
of our own time.

The hallmark of this attitude is its sense that the certitudes and
unshakable basic assumptions of former ages have been swept away, that they
have been tested and found wanting, that they have been discredited as cheap
and somewhat childish illusions. The decline of religious faith was masked
until the end of the Second World War by the substitute religions of faith in
progress, nationalism, and various totalitarian fallacies. All this was shattered
by the war. By 1942, Albert Camus was calmly putting the question why, since
life had lost all meaning, man should not seek escape in suicide. In one of the
great, seminal heart-searchings of our time, *The Myth of Sisyphus*, Camus tried
to diagnose the human situation in a world of shattered beliefs:

> A world that can be explained by reasoning, however faulty, is
> a familiar world. But in a universe that is suddenly deprived of
> illusions and of light, man feels a stranger. His is an irremediable
> exile, because he is deprived of memories of a lost homeland
> as much as he lacks the hope of a promised land to come. This
> divorce between man and his life, the actor and his setting, truly
> constitutes the feeling of Absurdity.[6]

'Absurd' originally means 'out of harmony', in a musical context.
Hence its dictionary definition: 'out of harmony with reason or propriety;
incongruous, unreasonable, illogical'. In common usage, 'absurd' may simply
mean 'ridiculous', but this is not the sense in which Camus uses the word,
and in which it is used when we speak of the Theatre of the Absurd. In an
essay on Kafka, Ionesco defined his understanding of the term as follows:
'Absurd is that which is devoid of purpose.... Cut off from his religious,
metaphysical, and transcendental roots, man is lost; all his actions become
senseless, absurd, useless.'[7] This sense of metaphysical anguish at the absurdity
of the human condition is, broadly speaking, the theme of the plays of Beckett,

Adamov, Ionesco, Genet, and the other writers discussed in this book. But it is not merely the subject-matter that defines what is here called the Theatre of the Absurd. A similar sense of the senselessness of life, of the inevitable devaluation of ideals, purity, and purpose, is also the theme of much of the work of dramatists like Giraudoux, Anouilh, Salacrou, Sartre, and Camus himself. Yet these writers differ from the dramatists of the Absurd in an important respect: they present their sense of the irrationality of the human condition in the form of highly lucid and logically constructed reasoning, while the Theatre of the Absurd strives to express its sense of the senselessness of the human condition and the inadequacy of the rational approach by the open abandonment of rational devices and discursive thought. While Sartre or Camus express the new content in the old convention, the Theatre of the Absurd goes a step further in trying to achieve a unity between its basic assumptions and the form in which these are expressed. In some senses, the *theatre* of Sartre and Camus is less adequate as an expression of the *philosophy* of Sartre and Camus—in artistic, as distinct from philosophic, terms—than the Theatre of the Absurd.

If Camus argued that in our disillusioned age the world has ceased to make sense, he did so in the elegantly rationalistic and discursive style of an eighteenth-century moralist, in well-constructed and polished plays. If Sartre argues that existence comes before essence and that human personality can be reduced to pure potentiality and the freedom to choose itself anew at any moment, he presents his ideas in plays based on brilliantly drawn characters who remain wholly consistent and thus reflect the old convention that each human being has a core of immutable, unchanging essence—in fact, an immortal soul. And the beautiful phrasing and argumentative brilliance of both Sartre and Camus in their relentless probing still, by implication, proclaim a tacit conviction that logical discourse can offer valid solutions, that the analysis of language will lead to the uncovering of basic concepts—Platonic ideas.

This is an inner contradiction that the dramatists of the Absurd are trying, by instinct and intuition rather than by conscious effort, to overcome and resolve. The Theatre of the Absurd has renounced arguing *about* the absurdity of the human condition; it merely *presents* it in being—that is, in terms of concrete stage images. This is the difference between the approach of the philosopher and that of the poet; the difference, to take an example from another sphere, between the *idea* of God in the works of Thomas Aquinas or Spinoza and the *intuition* of God in those of St. John of the Cross or Meister Eckhart—the difference between theory and experience.

It is this striving for an integration between the subject-matter and the form in which it is expressed that separates the Theatre of the Absurd from the Existentialist theatre.

It must also be distinguished from another important, and parallel, trend in the contemporary French theatre, which is equally preoccupied with the absurdity and uncertainty of the human condition: the 'poetic avant-garde' theatre of dramatists like Michel de Ghelderode, Jacques Audiberti, Georges Neveux, and, in the younger generation, Georges Schehadé, Henri Pichette, and Jean Vauthier, to name only some of its most important exponents. This is an even more difficult dividing line to draw, for the two approaches overlap a good deal. The 'poetic avant-garde' relies on fantasy and dream reality as much as the Theatre of the Absurd does; it also disregards such traditional axioms as that of the basic unity and consistency of each character or the need for a plot. Yet basically the 'poetic avant-garde' represents a different mood; it is more lyrical, and far less violent and grotesque. Even more important is its different attitude toward language: the 'poetic avant-garde' relies to a far greater extent on consciously 'poetic' speech; it aspires to plays that are in effect poems, images composed of a rich web of verbal associations.

The Theatre of the Absurd, on the other hand, tends toward a radical devaluation of language, toward a poetry that is to emerge from the concrete and objectified images of the stage itself. The element of language still plays an important part in this conception, but what *happens* on the stage transcends, and often contradicts, the *words* spoken by the characters. In Ionesco's *The Chairs*, or example, the poetic content of a powerfully poetic play does not lie in the banal words that are uttered but in the fact that they are spoken to an ever-growing number of empty chairs.

The Theatre of the Absurd is thus part of the 'anti-literary' movement of our time, which has found its expression in abstract painting, with its rejection of 'literary' elements in pictures; or in the 'new novel' in France, with its reliance on the description of objects and its rejection of empathy and anthropomorphism. It is no coincidence that, like all these movements and so many of the efforts to create new forms of expression in all the arts, the Theatre of the Absurd should be centred in Paris.

This does not mean that the Theatre of the Absurd is essentially French. It is broadly based on ancient strands of the Western tradition and has its exponents in Britain, Spain, Italy, Germany, Switzerland, Eastern Europe and the United States as well as in France. Moreover, its leading practitioners who live in Paris and write in French are not themselves Frenchmen.

As a powerhouse of the modern movement, Paris is an international rather than a merely French centre: it acts as a magnet attracting artists of all nationalities who are in search of freedom to work and to live nonconformist lives unhampered by the need to look over their shoulder to see whether their neighbours are shocked. That is the secret of Paris as the capital of the world's individualists: here, in a world of cafes and small hotels, it is possible to live easily and unmolested.

That is why a cosmopolitan of uncertain origin like Apollinaire; Spaniards like Picasso or Juan Gris; Russians like Kandinsky and Chagall; Rumanians like Tzara and Brancusi; Americans like Gertrude Stein, Hemingway, and E. E Cummings; an Irishman like Joyce; and many others from the four corners of the world could come together in Paris and shape the modern movement in the arts and literature. The Theatre of the Absurd springs from the same tradition and is nourished from the same roots. An Irishman, Samuel Beckett; a Rumanian, Eugène Ionesco; a Russian of Armenian origin, Arthur Adamov, not only found in Paris the atmosphere that allowed them to experiment in freedom, they also found there the opportunities to get their work produced.

The standards of staging and production in the smaller theatres of Paris are often criticized as slapdash and perfunctory. That may indeed sometimes be the case; yet the fact remains that there is no other place in the world where so many first-rate men of the theatre can be found who are adventurous and intelligent enough to champion the experimental work of new playwrights and to help them acquire a mastery of stage technique—from Lugné-Poë, Copeau, and Dullin to Jean-Louis Barrault, Jean Vilar, Roger Blin, Nicolas Bataille, Jacques Mauclair, Sylvain Dhomme, Jean-Marie Serreau, and a host of others whose names are indissolubly linked with the rise of much that is best in the contemporary theatre.

Equally important, Paris also has a highly intelligent theatre-going public, which is receptive, thoughtful, and as able as it is eager to absorb new ideas. This does not mean that the first productions of some of the more startling manifestations of the Theatre of the Absurd did not provoke hostile demonstrations or, at first, play to empty houses. What matters is that these scandals were the expression of passionate concern and interest, and that even the emptiest houses contained enthusiasts articulate enough to proclaim loudly and effectively the merits of the original experiments they had witnessed.

Yet in spite of these favourable circumstances, inherent in the fertile cultural climate of Paris, the success of the Theatre of the Absurd, achieved within a short span of time, remains one of the most astonishing aspects of this astonishing phenomenon. That plays so strange and puzzling, so clearly devoid of the traditional attractions of the well-made drama, should within less than a decade have reached the stages of the world from Finland to Japan, from Norway to the Argentine, and that they should have stimulated a large body of work in a similar convention, are in themselves powerful and entirely empirical tests of the importance of the Theatre of the Absurd.

The study of this phenomenon as literature, as stage technique, and as a manifestation of the thinking of its age must proceed from the examination of the works themselves. Only then can they be seen as part of an old tradition that may at times have been submerged but that can be traced back to antiquity.

Only after the movement of today has been placed within its historical context can an attempt be made to assess its significance and to establish its importance and the part it has to play within the pattern of contemporary thought.

A public conditioned to an accepted convention tends to receive the impact of artistic experiences through a filter of critical standards, of predetermined expectations and terms of reference, which is the natural result of the schooling of its taste and faculty of perception. Thus framework of values, admirably efficient in itself, produces only bewildering results when it is faced with a completely new and revolutionary convention—a tug of war ensues between impressions that have undoubtedly been received and critical preconceptions that clearly exclude the possibility that any such impressions could have been felt. Hence the storms of frustration and indignation always caused by works in a new convention.

It is the purpose of this book to provide a framework of reference that will show the works of the Theatre of the Absurd within their own convention so that their relevance and force can emerge as clearly to the reader as *Waiting for Godot* did to the convicts of San Quentin.

NOTES

1. *San Quentin News*, San Quentin, Calif, 28 November 1957.

2. ibid.

3. *Theatre Arts*, New York, July 1958.

4. ibid.

5. *San Quentin News*, 28 November 1957.

6. Albert Camus, *Le Mythe de Sisyphe* (Paris: Gallimard, 1942), p. 18.

7. Eugène Ionesco, '*Dans les armes de la ville*', *Cahiers de la Compagnie Madeleine Renaud Jean-Louis Barrault*, Paris, no. 20, October 1957.

KATHERINE H. BURKMAN

The Nonarrival of Godot:
Initiation into the Sacred Void

Albert Camus chose to return to an ancient myth for his definition of the modern hero of the absurd. Punished as all men since Adam have been for aspiring to the knowledge and immortality reserved for gods, Camus's Sisyphus takes up his task in the underworld of repeatedly and eternally rolling a huge stone up a mountain from which it repeatedly and eternally descends. This senseless and futile task becomes an image of bondage more potent, perhaps for contemporary society than the image of the rockbound, suffering Prometheus, one of Robert Brustein's prototypes of the messianic hero in modern drama.[1] Prometheus may rage against the gods with the courage of foresight—he sees the end of his ordeal—but Sisyphus must accept his ordeal as final, only rising above it on the wings of irony and the dry mock. "There is no fate," Camus states "that cannot be surmounted by scorn" and "one must imagine Sisyphus happy."[2]

If Camus has defined the possibilities for the absurd hero in terms of myth, Samuel Beckett has actually created a modern myth. Beckett's classical, absurdist play, *Waiting for Godot*, is not "... a burlesque of the biblical myth of redemption," although it may contain such burlesque: rather, "... The anti-myth built upon antiheroes rises from mere travesty to the elevated rank of a myth itself; from a work of art, it becomes an almost disassociated mythological symbol in its own right."[3]

From *The Arrival of Godot: Ritual Patterns in Modern Drama*, pp. 33–53. © Fairleigh Dickinson University Press, 1986.

The close relationship between myth, "a system of word symbols," and ritual, "a system of object and act symbols,"[4] has been explored both by anthropologists and by those "myth critics" who, following Sir James George Frazer and the Cambridge school of anthropologists, have explored the connections among myth, ritual, and art. Dismissing the debate about which comes first, the ritual or the myth, as irrelevant, anthropologist Clyde Kluckhohn notes that both myth and ritual are symbolic means of manipulating experience that man feels he cannot control. Noting their common psychological basis, Kluckhohn states:

> Ritual is an obsessive repetitive activity—often a symbolic dramatization of the fundamental "needs" of the society, whether "economic," "social," or "sexual." Mythology is the rationalization of those same needs, whether they are all expressed in overt ceremonial or not.[5]

The nonarriving Godot has taken his place beside Sisyphus, Prometheus, and other mythological figures of old, even as the nonacting characters in Beckett's play have provided the ritual basis of the Godot myth.

The two ways of suffering that are dramatized by Aeschylus in his *Prometheus Bound* reappear in *Waiting for Godot* and are seen, as in the earlier drama, to be both contrasting and similar. Like Prometheus bound to his rock, Didi and Gogo are bound to their place of appointment with Godot. Though their bondage may be more self-imposed than that of the rebellious Titan, it holds them just as surely as the adamantine chains that Hephaestus uses to bind him.

> ESTRAGON: Well, shall we go?
> VLADIMIR: Yes, let's go
> *They do not move.* (p. 35b)

Pozzo and Lucky's endless peregrinations may again seem more self-imposed than those of Prometheus's fellow-sufferer, Io, who is driven by the gadfly the jealous Hera has sent to punish her for her attractiveness to Zeus, but Pozzo and Lucky are not only tied to each other; they are bound to their endless journey. As in the ancient play, the contrasting forms of suffering in *Godot* are shown to be mere variations on the theme of the bondage of man, whether he is driven to stay or to go, a bondage that in the modern play, unlike the ancient, affords no certain, eventual deliverance.

There are, however, important differences as well as similarities in the sufferings of the four *Godot* characters. Although the play is seemingly lacking in action, its structure is a kind of initiation rite that its four major characters undergo with varying degrees of completion and success. All of them participate in the same rite and are involved in a general crisis of faith, but their resolutions to the crisis differ significantly. Mircea Eliade defines initiation as denoting "a body of ties and oral teachings whose purpose is to produce a decisive alteration in the religious and social status of the person to be initiated."[6] The *Godot* rite, however, is not the kind of puberty rite that Eliade describes "which introduces the candidate into the human community and into the world of spiritual and cultural value."[7] Beckett's drama reflects a world that has little human community and is all but devoid of spiritual and cultural value. Rather, the concern here is with those "specialized initiations" in which the individual attempts to transcend the human condition, ritual in its "metacultural and transhistorical" dimension during which the initiated undergoes "an existential experience—the experience of ritual death and the revelation of the sacred."[8]

The irony of the particular revelation of the sacred in *Waiting for Godot* lies in its location in what seems to be meaninglessness itself, the void. What the four major characters in Beckett's drama are involved in is an initiation rite that leads them to experience the void as sacred and to orient themselves accordingly. Pozzo's initiation begins in act 1 and is apparently completed between the acts so that in act 2 he becomes the shaman or initiatory guide for Vladimir, whose crisis of faith is at the center of the play. Lucky, who is something of an appendage to Pozzo, and Estragon, who is something of an appendage to Vladimir, take their roles in the initiation rite as well.

Pozzo's initiation or ritual death begins in act 1 with the gradual loss of his illusions of purpose and power. When he enters in circus-master fashion, driving Lucky, a rope around his neck, before him, Pozzo presents himself with such pomposity that Didi and Gogo momentarily mistake him for Godot. "I am Pozzo! (*Silence*) Pozzo! (*Silence.*) Does that name mean nothing to you? (*Silence*). I say does that mean nothing to you?" (p. 15b). Informing Didi and Gogo that they await Godot on "his" land, which he beneficently permits, "The road is free to all" (p. 16), he flaunts his many possessions, his watch, pipe, and vaporizer as well as those accessories which Lucky carries and furnishes on demand, such as a coat, whip, stool, and basket of food, chicken, and wine. He is clear, too, about his destination, the fair at which he plans to sell Lucky; and he has the wisdom to discourse on the twilight.

By the end of act 1, however, Pozzo has misplaced his pipe, vaporizer, and watch and has commented on the worn-out condition of both his whip and his memory. Unsure of himself, "I have such need of encouragement!" (p. 25b), he is sympathetic with the tramps as Godot worshipers—"I myself in your situation, if I had an appointment with a Godin ... Godet ... Godot ... anyhow you see who I mean, I'd wait till it was black night before I gave up" (p. 24)—but is also aware of the impending descent of black night that will make Godot's arrival irrelevant. Hanging on desperately, if comically, to an idea of secular time, he denies Vladimir's contention that time has stopped—"Whatever you like, but not that" (p. 24b)—but when he proceeds with assurance to offer his thoughts on the twilight they all inhabit, he soon falters. Combining the lyrical with the prosaic, he ends with an intuition of the gloom of night's sudden descent: "That's how it is on this bitch of an earth" (p. 25b).

All loss need not, of course, be initiatory, but Pozzo's attachment to his possessions makes the loss of some and the failure of others to work akin to the dismemberment ordeals that often accompany initiations, whether in puberty rites or as part of the initiation of a shaman. (Eliade gives numerous examples in which Shamans tell of their dreams of or experience of dismemberment by demons, a dismemberment symbolic of the death to the secular that precedes rebirth into the sacred.[9]) His role as Lucky's master is apparently also part of Pozzo's ordeal, for he sees this former "angel" as a demon. Sobbing, Pozzo complains, "He used to be so kind ... so helpful ... and entertaining ... my good angel ... and now ... he's killing me" (p. 23). The nature of the "death" he undergoes at Lucky's hands may be detected during Lucky's "think" speech in which he offers a vision of the wisdom of the ages become incoherent in the face of a universe that is wasting away, the single surety being that man too "wastes and pines wastes and pines" (p. 29). Pozzo's suffering increases during the speech, until he conspires with the others to stop Lucky by grabbing his hat on which he proceeds to trample: "There's an end to his thinking!" (p. 30).

The climactic loss, the descent of "black night," happens between the acts and we only hear about it, Pozzo's blindness and Lucky's muteness, as already accomplished in act 2. The properties that Lucky carried have now turned to sand, as have all the illusions of power or knowledge that had lingered in the former act.

Several critics have associated Pozzo's loss of sight with a concurrent loss of spiritual insight. Richard Schechner, for example, considers Pozzo's epiphany on time to be false. Prodded by Vladimir about when he lost his sight, Pozzo proclaims,

> Have you not done tormenting me with your accursed time! One day, is that not enough for you, one day he went dumb, one day I went blind, one day we'll go deaf, one day we were born, one day we shall die, the same day, the same second, is that not enough for you? (*Calmer.*) They give birth astride of a grave, the light gleams an instant, then it's night once more. (*He jerks the rope.*) On! (p. 57b)

"The experience of the play," Schechner suggests, "shows that there is plenty of time, too much; waiting means more time than things to fill it."[10] Curtis

M. Brooks also finds this second-act discourse on time to be a failure of perception and calls it "anti-mythic." Pozzo, he claims, is lost in profane time, which like him moves "on" but without a direction or sacred center to give it meaning.[11]

On the contrary. The insight to which Pozzo moves may be harrowing but it is not false; rather, it is the true epiphany of the play, a glimpse into the sacred void. Enter Sisyphus!

The theories of Mircea Eliade on time are most helpful here; he relates that religious man from the most primitive to the most sophisticated tends to experience the duration of time in which he lives historically, moment by moment, as profane, and the time of the creation of the world and all its inhabitants, which is a reversible time or "a primordial mythical time made present," as sacred. Religious festivals and rites evoke man's participation in this sacred time, which is transcendental and revelatory of reality.[12]

> Hence religious man lives in two kinds of time, of which the more important, sacred time, appears under the paradoxical aspect of a circular time, reversible and recoverable, a sort of eternal mythical present that is periodically reintegrated by means of rites. This attitude in regard to time suffices to distinguish religious from non-religious man; the former refuses to live solely in what, in modern terms, is called the historical present; he attempts to regain a sacred time that, from one point of view, can be homologized to eternity.[13]

In the second act Pozzo does, indeed, seem to be lost in profane time. Shorn of his illusions of purpose and power, Pozzo no longer seeks to sell Lucky at a fair,[14] but merely goes "on."

VLADIMIR: Where do you go from here?
POZZO: On. . . .
VLADIMIR: What is there in the bag?
POZZO: Sand. (*He jerks the rope.*) On!
VLADIMIR: Don't go yet.
POZZO: I'm going.
VLADIMIR: What do you do when you fall far from help?
POZZO: We wait till we can get up. Then we go on. On!
　(p. 57)

Not only does he merely go "on," as Sisyphus does, in futile fashion; his bag, formerly filled with food, contains sand, a good counterpart to Sisyphus's rock. In act 1 he had said that if he had an appointment with Godot, he would wait until "black night" before going on. In act 2 there is no mention by Pozzo of Godot. Black night has come to stay.

Despite total rejection of that eternity which Eliade finds an essential part of the religious experience, a hereafter in which man's suffering has meaning, Pozzo, like Sisyphus, it seems to me, has found a solution to his religious yearnings. Eliade says that the most secular of men revert to the religious quest for the sacred, though they do it in personal terms; and for secular man, too, time has different intensities.[15] Pozzo acts in true mythical fashion when he offers his vision of primal beginnings. And though that vision allows man's life as but a moment between life and death, that moment becomes sacred and hence, paradoxically, endless. As all time becomes "the same day," profane time is destroyed with whatever Godots may wait in the wings. When Pozzo says that "the blind have no notion of time, the things of time are hidden from them too" (p. 55b), he is not, as Brooks claims, denying the blind Tiresias's prophetic vision;[16] he is, rather, declaring secular time to be irrelevant. Like Hamm in Beckett's *Endgame*, who notes that "The end is in the beginning and yet you go on" (p. 69), Pozzo accepts death and nothingness and goes on in the face of it.

Pozzo comes close to Camus's idea of the absurd hero in his ability to go on in the face of an absurd, unknowable world. "The struggle itself toward the heights is enough to fill a man's heart," Camus says; "one must imagine Sisyphus happy."[17] But if Pozzo remains undefeated in the face of the void, passing through his initiation to the "sacred," to what is "real," he does not share Sisyphus's joy in life's futile struggle. Sisyphus retains something of the traditional rebel-victim's victory of mind over matter.[18] But mind—in this instance Lucky—remains an encumbrance to Pozzo, who has given up hope of selling him. Pozzo is doubtless consoled that Lucky is at least dumb—one remembers how he suffered through his "think" speech in act 1—but he does not take kindly to their mutual dependence, still calling him "pig" and "menial." If Estragon can't raise Lucky by pulling on the rope, Pozzo recommends giving "him a taste of his boot, in the face and the privates as far as possible" (p. 56).

As absurd hero and prophet, Pozzo is far more furious than joyful, and we see that fury exhibited in his climactic speech in which he finds Vladimir's questions about time "abominable" (p. 57). But the abominations of time are now Vladimir's, not his. "Have you not done tormenting me with *your* [my italics] accursed time?" (p. 57b). Profane time, Vladimir's, has become meaningless in the light of Pozzo's insight about sacred time as an instant between birth and death, an insight he delivers when "*calmer*," if not calm.

It is important that Vladimir shares Pozzo's epiphany, and that he is initiated into the mystery of the sacred void, because Pozzo, although he may come closest as a character to Camus's absurd hero, is not Beckett's. The wavering, doubt-ridden, backsliding Estragon and Vladimir are Beckett's anti-heroic heroes, and Pozzo and Lucky, who are far less sympathetic in their master–slave relationship than the tramps in their friendship or "bad marriage," share in that heroism only to the extent that they share in the quest for salvation and, on one level of the play's action, are but parts of a four-sided character.[19]

"Astride of a grave and a difficult birth," Vladimir remarks, picking up Pozzo's birth imagery after Pozzo and Lucky's exit. "Down in the hole, lingeringly, the grave-digger puts on the forceps. We have time to grow old. The air is full of our cries . . ." (pp. 58–58b). Although Vladimir may seem to refute Pozzo's vision,[20] since for him life's fleeting moment seems painfully long, he actually shares it and elaborates on it. As Jacques Dubois suggests, "Beckettian man, like Pascalian man, is torn between two infinities: a very short life in view of his appetite for living and a very long life because of his suffering."[21] Beckett noted in his book on Proust that there are moments of transition in which "the boredom of living is replaced with the suffering of being."[22] Like most initiations, which are transitions, what is involved is not just death, but rebirth.

The death-rebirth agonies of the *Godot* initiation rite involve the four characters in much confusion about time, place, and identity. "So there you are again," Vladimir remarks to Estragon at their opening of the play reunion. "Am I?", Estragon asks (p. 7). Pozzo does not recognize the tramps from meeting to meeting, nor does he know when he went blind, and Didi and Gogo are not sure of the place or time of their appointment with Godot, or of his identity. The various kinds of disorientation that Didi and Gogo and Pozzo and Lucky experience are clearly a part of the mutual religious crisis they are undergoing, but they just as clearly and ironically mark their progress in the initiation rite with which they are unwittingly involved.

Estragon, who seems least aware of what he is doing, where he is, and why, is at the outset really the farthest along of the four. He knows from the beginning that which the others learn by the end: "Nothing to be done" (p. 7). While Vladimir tends to intellectualize and ponder metaphysical questions, Estragon seems to intuit the nature of their predicament more profoundly, even though he may seem, like many a wise fool before him, to be merely slow-witted. Vladimir still works with a traditional sense of justice—if Estragon is beaten nightly, he must have done something to deserve it—but Estragon, in the manner of Camus's absurd hero, is quite convinced of his innocence.[23] When Vladimir suggests they might repent, Estragon goes to the heart of the matter. "Our being born?" he asks (p. 8b). Vladimir responds with that painful laugh which apparently relates to his physical condition, something to do with his bladder, but which, like all that is physical in the play, has its metaphysical dimension.

VLADIMIR: You'd make me laugh if it wasn't prohibited.
ESTRAGON: We've lost our rights?
VLADIMIR: (*distinctly*). We got rid of them. (p. 13)

Vladimir's is the more acute insight here. Indeed, Estragon's disorientation about time and place is not always a sign of his further progress; Vladimir sometimes catches up or surpasses him. And, as in the case of their repenting being born, they can share the wisdom of a bad joke. The point is that disorientation to profane time and place is not as negative as it seems; it often suggests a reorientation to time and place and an approach to the sacred void into which Pozzo has gazed with his blind eyes.[24]

The initiation in the play involves coming to terms not only with the nothingness (nothing to be done) of the human predicament, but with the nowhereness as well. When Vladimir asks Estragon if he doesn't recognize the place of their meeting in act 2, Estragon responds with fury. "Recognize! What is there to recognize? All my lousy life I've crawled about in the mud! And you talk to me about scenery! (*Looking wildly about him.*) Look at this muck heap! I've never stirred from it!" (p. 39). Slightly later, when Vladimir asks him where they were the evening before, Estragon responds, "How would I know? In another compartment. There's no lack of void" (p. 42). Estragon's inability to recognize their place of meeting is again a measure of his progress; he has already given up scenery as a mere coverup of the void that he has experienced as the essential reality.

Of course, such a perception of place as void seems antimythical in Eliade's terms since sacred place as well as sacred time involves a transcendent reality that gives form to chaos, while Estragon's angry recognition of the void suggests an inversion—the form of chaos is all the shape that there is. Just as Brooks sees Pozzo as lost in profane time, he sees the tramps as lost in profane space. "Vladimir and Estragon," he writes, "are tired pilgrims of the long and dusty way, which ordinarily leads from death, to life, from man to divinity, from time to timelessness. The play derives its power from its ironic implication that the road leads nowhere."[25] The point once again is, however, that the recognition that the road leads nowhere makes of nowhere the sacred center of the void itself; hence nowhere and notime become the very "atemporal mythic moment" that is sacred. Expressing concern with the separateness of chaos and form in art, Beckett has stated that the artist's "task" today is "to find a form that accommodates the mess."[26] "Can you make no use of nothing, nuncle?" the Fool asks Lear, who like the *Godot* tramps undergoes that initiation into nothingness, that acquaintance with himself as unaccommodated man that gives tragic shape, form, and meaning to nothingness.

Just as Estragon in some ways is farther along than Vladimir in the initiation into the sacred void, so Lucky is in some ways further along than

Pozzo. Lucky has already, Pozzo tells the tramps in the first act, taught Pozzo all the "beautiful" things he knows; and in his "think" speech, which Pozzo suffers as part of his own initiation, Lucky offers the half-mad babbling that is the result of his own experience of the abyss, the nothingness of the void. Lucky, who embodies the dying certainties of past civilization in act 1, seems in his muteness to embody death itself in act 2,[27] so that Pozzo, who is tied first to the dying and then to Death itself, comes to accept the burden of his own mortality, even though he continues to despise that burden.

Although Pozzo acts in the course of the second act as an initiatory guide, the prophet who announces the doom Estragon has intuited and Vladimir so fears, the tramps are attracted to Lucky's resolution to his religious crisis, the embracing of his slavery. If, as Vladimir suggests when he finds laughter painful, they have not lost their rights but have given them up, then they are more like Lucky in his voluntary slavery than is immediately apparent—first on the road rather than left in his dignity to die with the orchard. Estragon, who despairs whenever he is reminded by Vladimir that they must wait for Godot, would prefer the physical bondage of Lucky, who gets the bones, to the existential anguish of his waiting for an uncertain fate. At one point he even seems interested in taking Lucky's place.

> ESTRAGON: (*to Vladimir*) Does he want to replace him?
> VLADIMIR: What?
> ESTRAGON: Does he want someone to take his place or not?
> VLADIMIR: I don't think so.
> ESTRAGON: What?
> VLADIMIR: I don't know.
> ESTRAGON: Ask him. (p. 23)

And despite his tendency to dominate Estragon, Vladimir would also like to be the secure slave, although he finds he cannot think or dance on command.

> VLADIMIR: Tell me to think.
> ESTRAGON: What?
> VLADIMIR: Say, Think, pig!
> *Silence.*
> VLADIMIR: I can't!
> ESTRAGON: That's enough of that.
> VLADIMIR: Tell me to dance.
> ESTRAGON: I'm going. (p. 47)

Despite the attractiveness of the slave's role to Didi and Gogo, it is not their choice. Unable to close themselves off, in Lucky's fashion, from the moment of transition in which they seem to dwell, with all its openness to suffering and consciousness, they do not elect his kind of living death, any more than they elect the suicidal death with which they flirt in both acts, the hanging of themselves from the tree. Though they wistfully recall an earlier time when they might have been well enough dressed to ascend the Eiffel Tower and jump, and though Estragon fondly remembers a past suicide attempt in which he was saved from drowning by Vladimir, a time of symbolic rebirth,[28] like Camus's absurd hero the tramps reject that which "engulfs" or "settles" the absurd.[29]

Somewhat less heroic than Camus's absurd hero, however, who rejects death as an escape, Didi and Gogo reject suicide partly because death is as uncertain to them as life. Unsure of their weight—they don't know which one is heavier—they fear that whichever one is heavier will not succeed in hanging himself without breaking the bough. Like so many subsequent Beckett protagonists, all descended from Hamlet with his fears of an unknown hereafter, Didi and Gogo do not, like Pozzo in his epiphany, perceive a great nothingness in death. Haunted by "all the dead voices," who they say "talk about their lives," they surmise that "To have lived is not enough for them," though "To be dead is not enough for them" either (p. 40b).

Nor is Godot enough for the tramps. Although they do not reject Godot in any more final way than they reject suicide, again falling somewhat short of Camus's hero, who considers but rejects both suicide and God, their feelings toward Godot are deeply ambivalent. Vladimir views Godot as someone who will somehow change their lives—"Estragon: And if he comes? Vladimir: We'll be saved" (p. 606)—and who will punish them if they leave; but he is a figure whose possible arrival terrifies Estragon and whose off-stage actions as described by the messenger toward the end of each act seem as arbitrary as those of the Christian God, whom, with his white beard, he apparently resembles. Like the personal God in Lucky's "think" speech, who loves us dearly, Godot would seem to care—he sends his messenger with vague promises; but, as with Lucky's God and Vladimir's Christ and the two thieves, there are seemingly arbitrary exceptions to that love, which paradoxically comes from "the heights of divine apathia divine athambia divine aphasia" (p. 28b). Lucky's God, like Didi and Gogo's Godot, for reasons unknown, allows man to waste and pine. The failure of Godot as a savior is no doubt also partly a reflection of Estragon and Vladimir's perception of him. They do not quite know what they want from Godot or who he is and thus reduce him in their imagination to a businessman who must consult family, friends, agents, correspondents, books, and bank account before making a decision about how to help them.

Unable to rest in Lucky's stance, nor to make do with Godot, Vladimir comes to a crisis of faith at the play's climax[30] that Estragon experiences before and after him. Led by Pozzo as initiatory guide to the brink of the abyss, Vladimir undergoes the play's central initiation into the sacred void, exploring as part of that experience the mysterious relationship of life to death. Pozzo noted that when he woke up one day "blind as fortune," he wondered if he had awakened. "Sometimes I wonder if I'm not still asleep" (p. 55b). Vladimir picks up his image after he has left.

> VLADIMIR: Was I sleeping, while the others suffered? Am I sleeping now? To-morrow, when I wake, or think I do, what shall I say to to-day? That with Estragon my friend, at this place, until the fall of night, I waited for Godot? That Pozzo passed, with his carrier, and that he spoke to us? Probably. But in all that what truth will there be? (*Estragon, having struggled with his boots in vain, is dozing off again. Vladimir looks at him.*) He'll know nothing. He'll tell me about the blows he received and I'll give him a carrot. (*Pause.*) Astride of a grave and a difficult birth. Down in the hole, lingeringly, the grave-digger puts on the forceps. We have time to grow old. The air is full of our cries. (*He listens.*) But habit is a great deadener. (*He looks again at Estragon.*) At me too someone is looking, of me too someone is saying, He is sleeping he knows nothing, let him sleep on. (*Pause.*) I can't go on! (*Pause.*) What have I said? (pp. 58–58b)

Vladimir's epiphany, unlike Pozzo's, is not an angry statement but an exploration of the levels of reality in his world. He has questioned Pozzo's blindness, for unlike Godot's messenger boy, Pozzo seems to see him—"I wonder is he really blind … it seemed to me he saw us," (pp. 57b–58)—and to give him the sense of his own reality and identity that he has felt missing from his encounters with Godot's emissary. When Estragon asks him if Pozzo might not have been Godot, Vladimir is no longer sure.

> VLADIMIR: Not at all (*Less sure.*) Not at all! (*Still less sure.*) Not at all! (p. 58)

Vladimir questions, in Prospero fashion, the reality of his world, its truth or meaning. Of what does that world consist? A faithful waiting for Godot, blows for Estragon, friendship, death, the alleviation of suffering through habit. Placing Godot in the wings on one side, and death in the wings on the other, Vladimir's initiation involves a vision in which he brings the two face to face. Looking at the now sleeping Estragon, whose nightmares he has refused throughout the play to hear, he concludes his epiphany with a declaration of his own profound ignorance. "At me too someone is looking, of me too someone is saying, he is sleeping, he knows nothing, let him sleep on" (p. 586). It is as if he has been able, through his initiatory confrontation with death, to move outside of himself and observe himself from another perspective. Unlike Pozzo, however, who can go on in the face of the unknowableness of life, Vladimir says, "I can't go on" (p. 586). As surely as Oedipus comes to know the deeds he has done and the self that he is, Vladimir comes to know that he will never possess his deeds or know himself—that whether Godot or death comes, he must share the darkness that Pozzo inhabits. But the rebirth that initiation is all about and that Pozzo has experienced, eludes him.

Shortly before Vladimir's crisis of faith, Estragon suggests he cannot go on—"But I can't go on like this" (p. 44)—and he echoes himself and Vladimir toward the play's end when he again says, "I can't go on like this" (p. 60b). Far less devoted to their waiting situation than Vladimir, Estragon has made repeated attempts throughout the play to leave and has questioned the wisdom of their union several times, putting forth the possibility that they were not meant for the same road and noting with dismay that Vladimir sings when absent from his friend. It is Estragon, too, who has belittled Vladimir's faith. "We are not Saints but we have kept our appointment. How many people can boast as much?" Vladimir asks. "Billions" (p. 51b), is Estragon's deflating response. But Vladimir, who has been initiated into the mysteries of nothingness, is drawn back from the abyss into his hopes of salvation by Godot's messenger, and his response to Estragon's final "I can't go on like this" is "That's what you think" (p. 60b). If one were to evaluate Vladimir at this point in terms of Camus's absurd hero, one would have to say that he falters—that he returns to illusions about a transcendental future and to flirtation with suicide, an embrace of the enemy, death; they plan to bring some good rope for the purpose the next day.

As already noted, however, Vladimir is not Camus's hero but Beckett's absurdly antiheroic one. Opting for survival, like Pozzo he will go on; but going on, as Pozzo does, without hope of finding greater meaning in life's fleeting moment is not possible for Vladimir. "What they seek to complete," Michael Robinson writes of Didi and Gogo, "is the arbitrary series begun by birth, to reach that end where time is no more and where their present unreality is changed into certainty of their own identity and existence. What, in fact, they seek is to be reunited with the Self they know must exist outside time in the union of their personal infinity with that of the timeless void.[31] Pozzo may be able to make do with the flicker of life in the timeless void, but Vladimir insists on the Self. "Tell him you saw me" (p. 59), he says, almost attacking the messenger boy with his insistence on his own reality and significance.

Because the images of God are so unsatisfactory in the play, whether they are Lucky's or Didi and Gogo's, one is tempted to agree with those critics who suggest that Beckett knows full well that Godot will never come.[32]

Beckett does not, however, deride the now shaky faith of his hero. Rather, he undercuts Pozzo as hero, not only by keeping the master/slave relationship alive between Lucky and him, but also by giving the dead landscape some life, the leaves that appear overnight on the once-dead tree, by providing the agonized Estragon with new boots that fit better, a minor miracle in a world of decay and loss, and above all by sending the messenger boy in with Godot's message of promised future arrival. The stage as microcosm, the "board" (p. 55b) that Pozzo thinks they may be on, is not the "board" for Pozzo because it has a tree; his stage as microcosm is now totally barren. It is, however, the board for Vladimir and Estragon and for the audience who see the tree, who still look to the tree for its promise of the means to suicide or further life, and who relate to the wings from which Godot sends in his messenger and his message of hope.

The Parable of the Door in Franz Kafka's novel *The Trial* may not be the parable of this play, but it offers a useful parallel to the *Godot* situation. Joseph K., condemned to death for unknown crimes, hears the parable from a priest who would instruct him. The door in the parable, which presumably leads to some higher truth or sacred order, is guarded so that the man for whom it is held open may not enter. The guard, however, tells the man who has never entered, just as he closes it, that it was strictly for him. Salvation in Kafka is improbable and remote; the messengers of the higher power are themselves corrupt or seem, like the guard at the door, to withhold salvation rather than offer it. Joseph K., unresigned to Pozzo's vision of life as a flash in the great void, dies like a dog, feeling justly that in his year's "trial" he has not gained much insight. He has not even tried to get past the guard.

Godot's messenger is not corrupt; he is an innocent, who does not understand his master's inclinations, why he is favored over his brother, and he does not recognize Didi and Gogo from day to day. Vladimir's second meeting with him near the play's end, in which he gives the boy's answers for him, suggests Vladimir's increased doubt. He has learned from Pozzo and from his own experience, and if he merely repeated what he now must feel is an all but hopeless litany, an empty ritual of hope deferred in which the words are there, but not the music, then one might say his initiation into the mysteries of death and the void were complete and he could take up Lucky's bags of sand or approach Sisyphus's rock. But Vladimir backs off from the initiation rite he has undergone.

> BOY: What am I to tell Mr. Godot, Sir?
> VLADIMIR: Tell him ... (*he hesitates*) ... tell him you saw me and that ... (*he hesitates*) ... that you saw me. (*Pause. Vladimir advances, the Boy recoils. Vladimir halts, the Boy halts. With sudden violence.*) You're sure you saw me, you won't come and tell me to-

> morrow that you never saw me! *Silence. Vladimir makes a sudden spring forward, the Boy avoids him and exits running.* ... (p. 59)

His insistence on the reality of the self and on being perceived[33] is the message Vladimir sends back. The possibility that spring may come again, that the wasteland may be redeemed, that it is significant that one of the thieves was saved, that this is not a Dantesque Inferno ("Estragon: I'm in hell") in which hopeless repetition of suffering is the order, but a purgatorial passage to a renewed and more meaningful existence remains.

The juxtaposition of the two orientations to salvation, Didi and Gogo waiting for Godot and Pozzo and Lucky going on in the face of nothingness, is conflated in Vladimir, who is initiated into the latter but chooses the former. Indeed, what one sees by play's end is that the two attitudes are not as opposite as they seem. They are juxtaposed in Estragon's attitudes as well as in Vladimir's, for Estragon sees himself one moment as a Christ figure, the next as utterly impotent. Having left his boots at the end of act 1 for another person with smaller feet, Estragon shocks Vladimir with his suggestion that, like Christ, he can go barefoot.

> ESTRAGON: All my life I've compared myself to him.
> VLADIMIR: But where he lived it was warm, it was dry!
> ESTRAGON: Yes. and they crucified quick.
> *Silence.*
> VLADIMIR: We've nothing more to do here.
> ESTRAGON: Nor anywhere else. (p. 34b)

Only a silence separates Estragon's perception of himself as a scapegoat, the counterpart to Lucky, whose dance is the "scapegoat's agony," from his perception of himself as totally ineffectual, lost in profane time and space.

Mircea Eliade begins his book *The Sacred and Profane* by alluding to Rudolf Otto's 1917 publication *Das Heilige* (*The Sacred*) in which he deals with God as a "terrible *power.*" Numinous experiences for Otto are terrifying because they are inhuman in their otherness and fullness and make man feel his impotence and nothingness.[34] The sense of their own nothingness in the scheme of things, whether that scheme allows us Pozzo's moment in the infinite void, a void which has become more numinous by play's end than the Godot who might save man from it, or whether that scheme allows us Godot, whose own impotence—he does nothing—seems a magnification of their own, is something that Pozzo and Lucky and Vladimir and Estragon share. Nowhere is their unity clearer than when they are all piled up on the ground in act 2 in a helpless heap that demonstrates their shared inability to help each other or themselves.

Still, if one considers the fall of the *Godot* four as part of their initiatory ordeal, one may see some positive aspects in it. They become much like Victor W. Turner's "threshold people," or "liminal personae," who, like neophytes in initiation ceremonies, lack possessions and status or anything "that may distinguish them from their fellow neophytes or initiands."[35] Stripped of his possessions and sight, Pozzo on the ground answers Estragon when he calls out both Abel and then Cain. He has become, Estragon asserts ironically, "all humanity" (p. 54), and, in a sense, all four have so become. United on the ground, the *Godot* characters enter into a new kind of community, in Turner's vocabulary a "communitas," which can be a creative and humanizing transitory condition in which to be.

Then, too, they get up. Rising, clowns that they are, from what Pozzo earlier called this "bitch of an earth" (p. 25b), but Estragon now calls "Sweet mother earth" (p. 53), the four share a tremendous aptitude for survival, if not for salvation. Vladimir and Estragon really only play at suicide as they play at being the tree or being Pozzo and Lucky. Like Pozzo and Lucky, they go "on." The four characters are as resilient as all fools, those who get slapped and bounce back for more.

The two stances, that of going "on" in the face of nothingness and that of going on in terms of standing still or waiting for Godot to transform their lives, come together most clearly in Vladimir, but they are not fully integrated in him. As Robinson says, the tramps fail to unite the self's personal infinity outside of time, Godot's promised transformation of reality, "with that of the timeless void."[36] Or, as Eva Metman notes in her Jungian interpretation of the play, the dependence of the members of the couples on each other and Vladimir's dependence on Godot are stagnating. For Metman, "This inseparability of factors of potential conflict expresses a state of latency in the psyche."[37]

Giving up Godot may be the solution of several critics, but it is not Beckett's solution for the integration of fragmented characters or the fragmented psyche of modern man. If giving up Godot as an illusion were Beckett's solution, Pozzo would be his hero, a Pozzo reintegrated with his intellect, not still tied to it with a rope. That Beckett offers no solution is partly the key to the power of the Godot myth. Taking up Chekhov's dispossessed exiles on the road and Chekhov's ironical non-judging attitude, Beckett looks at those characters, unaccommodated man exposed to the elements, and finds that they have grown a bit more cruel than those of his mentor (excluding Natasha perhaps); Firs left behind is pathetic; Lucky on the road is both pathetic and vicious. Lopakhin orders the ax to fall but weeps for those he ousts and for himself; he feels as dispossessed by his achievement as those he dispossesses; Pozzo suggests only ill treatment for the slave from whom he has wrested power. But Beckett still provides us characters in *Waiting for*

Godot who, like Chekhov's, dream of a redeemed future, that which Godot will bring, one that is related to a more ideal past, a time when Lucky's thinking made sense and when the paradox of a personal God who cares and human suffering was resolved in some sense of justice.

This impulse to look backward and forward in Chekhov and Beckett rather than to the present is correctly perceived by Clayton A. Hubbs in his article "Chekhov and the Contemporary Theatre" as part of the playing out of the ritual drama of the year. "At the back of the plays [Chekhov's] is the ritual of the year drama and behind that the edenic myth of a lost paradise."[38] I have already explored elements of the year drama with its dying-reviving gods in Ibsen's *The Wild Duck* and O'Neill's *The Iceman Cometh* (see chapter 1), and Brooks has shown *Waiting for Godot* to be such a year drama, a battle between winter and spring in which winter remains in the ascendancy. "In the seasonal structure of the play," Hubbs says of *The Three Sisters*, "the action regresses, from spring to winter, from the promise of renewal to death."[39] Hubbs, however, mistakenly thinks that because Chekhov is a secular writer, he does not believe in the reality of his myth. "Chekhov's purpose," he writes, "is to bring about an awareness of myth's absence and the human consequences of the denial of the immediate material world. When that awareness occurs, one assumes that the characters would regain the ability to love and rediscover the 'true myth' of collective communion."[40]

Beckett, however, just like Estragon and Vladimir, does not *not* believe in Godot any more than Chekhov denies the validity of the aspiration of his various characters. While the ritual routines, the little "canters" or vaudeville exchanges of Vladimir and Estragon, may seem merely repetitious and empty of meaning, habit operating as the great deadener, they are rituals nevertheless; and they are done, not only to pass the time, but also to give themselves "the impression we exist" (p. 44b) and to influence Godot's arrival. At the same time that Estragon knows and Pozzo and Vladimir learn that there is nothing to be done, Vladimir and Estragon are not certain and continue to act. Estragon searches for causes in his boot, Vladimir in his hat. When they speak of the dead voices that they attempt to shut out with their conversation, Estragon hears them like the rustling of leaves, which he insists on repetitively in contrast and in conflict with Vladimir who hears them first like wings and sand and then like feathers and ashes (p. 40b). His new, better-fitting boots first appear to Estragon as brown and then "a kind of green" (p. 43b). When they "do the tree," upon which a few leaves have mysteriously appeared, imitating it by standing on one foot, they clearly do it as a ritual incantation to God, as if trying to merge with what little life the tree has in order to make God recognize them. "Do you think God sees me?" (p. 49b), Estragon asks Vladimir, as he staggers about imitating the tree, their desire for recognition and pity becoming desperate.

VLADIMIR: You must close your eyes.
Estragon closes his eyes, staggers worse.
ESTRAGON: (*Stopping, brandishing his fists, at the top of his voice*). God have pity on me!
VLADIMIR: (*vexed*). And me?
ESTRAGON: On me! On me! Pity! On me! (p. 49b)

At this point, the staggering Didi and Gogo once again confront the staggering Pozzo and Lucky, and the final series of ritual routines take place, in which the four fall and rise, each couple going "on" in its own way.

The rituals, as in Chekhov, are ineffectual. Just as the Cherry Orchard is not saved and the three sisters do not return to Moscow, so Godot does not arrive. But if they have failed as worshipers, Didi and Gogo have not failed enough.

VLADIMIR: This is becoming really insignificant.
ESTRAGON: Not enough. (p. 44)

From the beginning they have been waiting for Godot to come or night to fall. Night, the void, has fallen once toward the end of act 1 and once toward the end of act 2, has permanently fallen for the blinded Pozzo of act 2, and has been the spiritual environment or condition of their ongoing litany— "Nothing to be done." But if they have progressed toward accepting their lives as a second in the void, the tramps continue to hope for more.

In the final comic ritual routine, Vladimir returns to his role as straight man to Estragon's simpleton. Estragon's trousers have fallen as a result of removing his belt for a suicide attempt, and he is not aware that they are down. In his disorientation to secular space, there is no significant difference at any rate between up and down. Vladimir must remind him.

VLADIMIR: Pull on your trousers.
ESTRAGON: What?
VLADIMIR: Pull on your trousers.
ESTRAGON: You want me to pull off my trousers?
VLADIMIR: Pull ON your trousers.
ESTRAGON: (*realizing his trousers are down*). True. *He pulls up his trousers.*
VLADIMIR: Well? Shall we go?
ESTRAGON: Yes, let's go.
They do not move. (p. 60b)

As in act 1, even when night has fallen, Didi and Gogo do not move. The ending of the second act, which simply exchanges the speakers of the ending of act 1—"Estragon: Well, shall we go? Vladimir: Yes, let's go. *They do not move.*" (p. 35b)—is more powerful than the former conclusion, partly because the fallen trousers have left Estragon not only comic in his unawareness of his exposure, but more fully exposed. The dynamics of the couple's inaction have now been explored in more depth than they had been in act 1. Vladimir has undergone his initiation and has experienced a crisis of faith that Estragon, in a more diffuse way, has been undergoing throughout. In the light of that initiation rite, in which nothingness has taken on the shape of the sacred, the black void giving life's mythical moment its luminosity, even as a picture frame sets off the picture it encloses, the rituals the clowns have repeated to fill their time and to worship and summon Godot have become more desperate and doubtful.

I suggested earlier that the key to the power of the Godot myth was partly Beckett's refusal to offer solutions, to tell us whether Godot exists, who he is, or whether he will ever arrive. Significantly, Beckett has noted that the key word in his play is "perhaps."[41] The final lines, together with the characters' immobility, pull together all the strands of the play and ironically demonstrate the contemporary vitality of the Godot myth.

For Didi and Gogo to remain is absurd. The messenger boy has told them that Godot won't come today but will surely come tomorrow. His future arrival may be unsure, but they know he will not arrive today. They must take cover. Their immobility, then, cannot be taken as religious dedication ("They also serve who only stand and wait") so much as for inertia ("Habit is a great deadener") or despair ("I can't go on"). Because, however, the couple return each twilight to wait for Godot, their final stasis, logic aside, does also represent that immobility of waiting which is their form of worship. What we have at the end are two orientations to salvation that the play has explored, life as an atemporal moment in the void and life spent waiting for Godot, integrated in an image of stasis; Didi and Gogo's inability to end their slow crucifixion leaves them suspended in a state of despairing hope. They may not be strong enough to do otherwise, but they do also serve who only stand and wait.

Bound to his rock, Prometheus flings his defiance at Zeus's messengers, comforts the wandering Io as best he can with prophecies of eventual freedom for them both, and boasts that one of his gifts to man was blind hope. As a man-god, he must suffer for his knowledge and gifts, but he asserts himself and he feels free. Pushing his rock up the hill in futile labor, Sisyphus gives up the Promethean gift of blind hope and accepts his suffering as endless, but he finds joy in his scorn of what the gods inflict. By scorning the human condition as absurd, he rises above it, asserts himself, and feels free. Reclaiming the gift of blind hope, Didi and Gogo have given up the right to laugh. Although they, too, assert themselves—"Tell him you saw us"—they are not sure of their own existence or of the nature of Godot.

Why, then, overcome as we are today with a feeling of impotence, do we find Beckett's reflection of our predicament such a potent myth? Unlike Didi and Gogo, of course, we have not given up the right to laugh and we enjoy what Nietzsche called the "discharge of our nausea"[42] as we follow the antics of the four *Godot* clowns; also, despite the inefficacy of the rituals of the play, we cannot help but find in the resilience of these four, both hope for our own survival and a tragicomic assertion of self that, in Kafkaesque fashion, at least keeps the door of salvation open.

Perhaps we do not so much laugh at the *Godot* clowns as for them. As we observe the resilience with which they have handled their own potential despair, whether it be Lucky's persistence in his alleviating role of slave, Pozzo's dogged movement onward with his new, darker vision of reality, or Vladimir and Estragon's tragicomic assertion of self, we see a starkly comic anatomy of the ways in which we may persist in the modern world. And as Vladimir backs off from his initiation into the sacred void, we come to understand that he may be participating, along with Estragon, in some more mysterious initiation rite, a moment of transition in which "the boredom of living is replaced with the suffering of being,"[43] and from that moment, neither of them retreats.

NOTES

1. Brustein, *The Theatre of Revolt*, pp. 18–19.

2. Camus, *The Myth of Sisyphus*, pp. 90–91.

3. Gabor Mihalyi, "Beckett's 'Godot' and the Myth of Alienation," *Modern Drama* 9, no. 3 (December 1966): 329. See also Bert O. States, *The Shape of Paradox: An Essay on "Waiting for Godot,"* pp: 19–20. Discussing Beckett's biblical style, States suggests that "... Godot is not (like MacLeish's *J.B.* or Giraudoux's *Judith*) an old biblical myth in modern dress but a new myth, or story about the plight of modern man, in old dress; it is a parable for today, such as might appear in a latter-day Bible aimed at accommodating modern problems of despair and alienation."

4. Clyde Kluckhohn, "Myth and Ritual: A General Theory," in *Myth and Literature: Contemporary Theory and Practice*, ed. John B. Vickery, p. 39.

5. Ibid., pp. 43–44.

6. Mircea Eliade, *Rites and Symbols of Initiation: The Mysteries of Birth and Rebirth*, p. x.

7. Ibid., p. x.

8. Ibid., pp. 128–130.

9. Ibid., pp. 74, 90–91.

10. Richard Schechner, "Godotology: There's Lots of Time in *Godot*," *Modern Drama* 9, no. 3 (December 1966): 273.

11. Curtis M. Brooks, "The Mythic Pattern in *Waiting for Godot*," *Modern Drama* 9, no. 3 (December 1966): 298.

12. Mircea Eliade, *The Sacred and the Profane: The Nature of Religion*, p. 68.

13. Ibid., p. 70. In the Judeo-Christian tradition, Eliade explains, God does manifest his presence in historical moments that are not reversible, but here, too, historical time

will be abolished with the future arrival of the messiah (Judaism) or the second coming (Christianity) (pp. 110–13).

14. In the original French version of *Waiting for Godot*, the name of the fair at which Pozzo plans to sell Lucky in act 1 is *Saint-Sauveur*. The implication here is that in the second act Pozzo no longer seeks religious salvation in any traditional sense.

15. Eliade, *The Sacred and the Profane*, p. 71.

16. Brooks, "The Mythic Pattern in *Waiting for Godot*," p. 298.

17. Camus, *The Myth of Sisyphus*, p. 91.

18. Steven J. Rosen, *Samuel Beckett and the Pessimistic Tradition*, p. 47.

19. Several critics discuss the four characters as if, at least on one level, they are one. See, for example, Martin Esslin, *The Theatre of the Absurd*, p. 67, or Frederick Busi, *The Transformations of Godot*, p. 95. Busi discusses the play as a monodrama in which the four characters are Godot and have arrived.

20. Schechner, "Godotology," p. 273.

21. Jacques Dubois, "Beckett and Ionesco: The Tragic Awareness of Pascal and the Ironic Awareness of Flaubert," *Modern Drama* 9, no. 3 (December 1966): 290.

22. Samuel Beckett, *Proust*, p. 8.

23. Camus, *The Myth of Sisyphus*, p. 39. Speaking of the absurd hero, Camus writes, "He feels innocent. To tell the truth, that is all he feels—his irreparable innocence."

24. Bert O. States, in *The Shape of Paradox*, senses Beckett's mythical use of time in his discussion of Lucky's "think" speech. "I would argue, however," he writes, "that the impulse in a work to transcend the limits of finite time and space, in the right conditions, eventuates in myth and that we have the basics of such conditions in *Godot*; . . . this pell-mell madness (Lucky's speech) functions very much like amnesia in the Beckett universe: it releases the character from bondage to a sensuous and temporal world. Does it not, in fact, create the same liberty of inference, or free association, that we have in Shakespeare when 'mad' characters like Lear are set loose from society to conjure impossible nightmare worlds based crudely on the world of social fact? And could we not say that in such moments Shakespeare verges on the mythical?" (pp. 43–44). Oddly enough, States refutes his own point later in his otherwise fine interpretation of the play, when he discusses memory as a means to grace, whether in a "divinely ordained" world or a "humanistic" one, finding the cases of amnesia in the play to be an indication of "grace withheld" (p. 101).

25. Brooks, "The Mythic Pattern in *Waiting for Godot*," p. 295.

26. Quoted by David H. Hesla in his *The Shape of Chaos: An Interpretation of the Art of Samuel Beckett*, p. 7.

27. Sigmund Freud identifies muteness with death in his essay "The Theme of the Three Caskets," in *The Standard Edition of the Complete Psychological Works of Sigmund Freud*, 24 vols, trans. and ed. James Strachey, 12:301.

28. Water dreams, says Freud, often suggest birth, and dreams that involve rescue from water suggest giving birth (Sigmund Freud, *The Interpretation of Dreams*, pp. 435–37, 459).

29. Camus, *The Myth of Sisyphus*, pp. 40–41.

30. I take issue with those critics who deny the play any kind of Aristotelian structure or climax. Ramon Cormier and Janis L. Pallister, for example, in *Waiting for Death: The Philosophical Significance of Beckett's En Attendant Godot*, suggest that the play lacks conventional form. "His antiplay," they say of Beckett's *Godot*, "a dyptich containing a play-within-a-play, has no characterization and no traditional plot" (p. 3). If one grasps the play's ritual structure, the initiation rite in which the characters are involved, one may, it seems to me, see how the play, despite its actionless appearance, is actually structured, in part, in quite

traditional ways.

31. Michael Robinson, *The Long Sonata of the Dead: A Study of Samuel Beckett*, p. 244.

32. Gunther Anders, for example, says Beckett derides his characters' belief in Godot; Anders suggests that the play may deal with religion but is not itself religious ("Being without Time: On Beckett's Play *Waiting for Godot*," in *Samuel Beckett: A Collection of Critical Essays*, ed. Martin Esslin, p. 145).

33. Beckett's interest in George Berkeley and his dictum that "To be is to be perceived," has apparently been a major influence on his art. See Rosen, *Samuel Beckett and the Pessimistic Tradition*, pp. 166–68.

34. Eliade, *The Sacred and the Profane*, p. 10.

35. Victor Turner, *The Ritual Process: Structure and Anti-Structure*, p. 95.

36. Robinson, *The Long Sonata of the Dead*, p. 244.

37. Eva Metman, "Reflections on Samuel Beckett's Plays," in *Samuel Beckett: A Collection of Critical Essays*, ed. Martin Esslin, p. 132.

38. Clayton A. Hubbs, "Chekhov and the Contemporary Theatre," *Modern Drama* 24, no. 3 (September 1981): 360.

39. Ibid., p. 361.

40. Ibid., p. 364.

41. An interview with Beckett quoted by Alec Reid in *All I Can Manage, More Than / Could: An Approach to the Plays of Samuel Beckett*, p. 11.

42. Nietzsche, *The Birth of Tragedy*, p. 60. Neitzsche here defines the comic as the "artistic discharge of the nausea of absurdity."

43. Beckett, *Proust*, p. 8.

NORMAND BERLIN

The Tragic Pleasure of Waiting for Godot

Back in 1956, when I saw the New York production of *Waiting for Godot*, I didn't know Beckett from Adam. A friend of mine had heard that a strange play was being praised by some critics and damned by others, and he thought I would like to see it, so he bought the tickets, and we went. It was the most exhilarating evening I had had in the theater until then, and it remains so after thirty years of playgoing. Something happened to me while I was watching it, and at the time—while watching it, that is—I did not know what. I'm still not altogether sure, but I've spent a lot of time trying to find out why I felt the way I did. I remember that when the curtain descended on those frozen figures, Didi and Gogo, I too remained frozen for a few seconds before I joined in the applause for the actors—Bert Lahr, who played Gogo; E. G. Marshall, who played Didi; Kurt Kasznar, as Pozzo; Alvin Epstein, as Lucky. I left the theater in a kind of daze, I remember, not because of the obscurity of the play's meaning—that special academic daze would come later—but because of the sheer purity of the presentation. Something new was happening in theater, yet something deceptively simple. A road, a tree, two men talking and waiting for someone called Godot to come. The words they spoke, common words, sang out with a remarkable clarity, and yet they touched mystery; the very simplicity of presentation seemed to elicit strongly felt emotions. Beckett was drawing an uncannily deep response from the

From *Beckett at 80/Beckett in Context*, pp. 46–63. © 1986 by Oxford University Press.

often crazy juxtaposition of word, gesture, and silence. Like Keats, when he first looked into Chapman's Homer, I was affected by the "pure serene" of the play. Keats writes: "Then felt I like some watcher of the skies / When a new planet swims into his ken / Or like stout Cortez when with eagle eyes / He stared at the Pacific—and all his men / Looked at each other with a wild surmise / Silent, upon a peak in Darien." Something happened to me that New York evening of 1956 and, as we all know as we celebrate Beckett's eightieth birthday (which coincides with the thirtieth anniversary of that Broadway production of *Waiting for Godot*), something happened to modern drama. The play has become a touchstone, a modern classic that makes most other modern plays—and many plays not so modern—seem artistically insignificant. I left the theater that evening exhilarated; my friend left it annoyed, believing that he was the victim of an enormous hoax. Well, what was there about that evening, about that play both praised and damned, that gave me pleasure?—and that is the word I want, pleasure.

To answer such a question, I must first try to recall what happened at the performance, what happened to me as a spectator of a specific staging of the play on a particular night, which comes before any examination of what happens in the play, the more familiar academic and critical enterprise. What did I see and hear? What did I experience? It was a long time ago, but this is what I remember about that performance. I remember—am I reminding you of Krapp hearing his own tape?—I remember the curtain rising to Gogo's enormous and engrossing effort to take off his boot. Bert Lahr brilliantly presented a man's confrontation with an inanimate thing, his panting and his looks exhibiting pure exhaustion. His physical effort believably and inevitably led to words that rang out clearly: "Nothing to be done." I remember E. G. Marshall, as Didi, walking onstage stiffly with legs apart, and I knew the poor guy was having trouble with his groin. I remember Lahr periodically gazing in every direction, including the audience's, with hands screening his eyes, looking for something. I remember a lot of business with hats, not only Didi looking into his and tapping it but also the switching of hats and especially the hat that had to be taken off Lucky to stop his endless speech. I remember that speech—not its words, of course, but its delivery, interminable, exhausting, a tour de force by actor Alvin Epstein. And I think I remember my relief when it was over, a relief I shared with Didi and Gogo and Pozzo—and Lucky, too. I remember a lot of pacing around, a lot of movement, a lot of going around in circles but also movement across the stage, especially by Pozzo and Lucky, probably because that rope between them called attention to itself. (In a play of few props and no scenery, everything counts!) I remember the way Pozzo, whip in hand, loudly shouted "On!" to the burdened Lucky. I remember Lucky's quick and stiff dance, and Lahr's clumsy imitation of it. I remember a heap of bodies onstage, trying to get up, but stumbling. I remember Lahr eating a carrot with such eagerness and sucking the end of it so suggestively that I believed him when he said, "I'll never forget this carrot." I remember how cozily Gogo crawled up into himself to go to sleep and how tenderly Didi covered him with his own coat. I remember the buzzing of the audience in the beginning of act 2, when the three or four leaves on the previously bare tree were discovered. (This discovery by the audience came before Didi looked at the tree; after all, when a play's landscape is bare, even a leaf or two will cause a stir.) I remember Gogo's boots, left on center stage during the intermission, splayed Chaplin-style, staring at the audience as though they had become characters, too. And I'll never forgot the different ways that Bert Lahr said, "Ah!" with his finger in the air, when he was reminded that they were waiting for Godot, nor will I forget the frozen positions and glaring stares of Didi and Gogo as each act ended and the curtain descended.

That was a special evening, and as I look back on it, I realize that so much of the play's impact on me depended on its physical reality, on the gestures, on the few props (like hats and boots and carrots and rope), on the bareness of scene, on the sheer here-and-now of it. The life of the play seemed fully present to my senses, and that offered a kind of pleasure, despite the frustrations and sadnesses and pain that were dramatized. That is, the play got to me on the first level because Beckett permitted nothing to come between me and the stage. The experience was an experience in the theater—Beckett never allowing me to forget I was seeing a play—but strangely authentic as well, a kind of higher realism.

Of course, as I think back on these first impressions, as I try to perceive myself watching the play, I realize that other contexts must have helped to stir my emotions of the moment. These were the echoes produced by the physical images. How could two men wearing bowlers, two men who were annoyed with one another and dependent on one another, one self-important, the other a little obtuse, how could two such men not remind me of Laurel and Hardy? How could I not see Buster Keaton when Gogo gazed in all directions with hands screening eyes? How could I not see Chaplin when those boots were positioned in that splayed way on center stage? How could I not be reminded of the Marx Brothers' hat routine in *Duck Soup* when Didi and Gogo play with their hats? And, on the more serious side, how could the play's most important activity, or nonactivity, waiting—manifested both physically (as Didi and Gogo nervously paced the boards, listening, anxious to hear if someone were coming) and verbally (in the form of such an exchange as, "Let's go." "We can't." "Why not?" "We're waiting for Godot." "Ah!")—how could waiting, that characteristically frustrating daily experience, not elicit emotional responses that filled in the many silences of the play? How could I not—as part of a post-Holocaust audience—not think of all the homeless tramps, the uprooted wanderers, the dispossessed, when I saw the wretched

Lucky carrying a bag and walking so slowly, head down, across a desolate landscape? That image was reinforced, surely, by the loudness and corpulence of Pozzo, a master standing for that master race forever persecuting victims. In that context, how could ill-fitting boots—in fact, the very idea of boots, piles of boots—not recall Nazi concentration camps, where so much waiting was done? (It was much later that I was to learn that Beckett's Estragon was originally called Levy and that Beckett's close friend and fellow fighter in the Resistance, Alfred Péron, died as a result of his treatment by the Germans in the Mauthausen concentration camp.)

With time, with reading the play again and again, with teaching it, with seeing other performances, with reading the critics, the play has become richer for me; but now I'm more troubled with the play's meaning and troubled with what others believe to be the play's meaning and troubled with problems concerning the play's genre. The performance of 1956 seemed so clean, so pure, so accessible. Always I try to go back to those first stage images, those first impressions, in order to take a firm hold on the play lest I leave it too far behind to talk about its philosophy, to discuss absurdism or the stance of art against absurdism, to examine the play's comedy and the tragic implications of its comedy or the play's tragedy and the comic possibilities of its tragedy. These large considerations cannot be avoided because the play's provocativeness seems inexhaustible, which in one respect is not surprising because *Waiting for Godot* is a rich and great work of art, but in another respect is surprising because the stage images are so clear, the words (except for Lucky's speech) so understandable, the actions so elemental, the actors so exposed. The play has become such a puzzlement to critics that they (we) cannot even agree on whether anything is happening onstage. Vivian Mercier's much-quoted assertion that in *Godot* "nothing happens, twice" has a catchy Beckettian ring to it, but it is not altogether accurate. We may wish to argue whether the play has an action or a plot (and those who say no will probably win the argument), but something happens in *Godot*; in fact, many things happen. The play is filled with incidents. We may wish to assert exasperatedly with Guildenstern in Tom Stoppard's Beckettian play, "Incidents! All we get is incidents! Dear God, is it too much to expect a little sustained action?!" But incidents are happenings. It is precisely because some very important things happen that specific emotions are elicited from the audience. I wish to suggest that these are the emotions we associate with the genre of tragedy. *Waiting for Godot*—with Beckett's playfully erudite mind forever at work—derives from many traditions, most of them popular comic traditions, well documented by a number of scholars; but its effect is closer to tragic effect than to any other kind, and the pleasure it affords is what I would call "tragic pleasure."

"Nothing to be done." These are the play's first words, the words that seem to set the tone for the play that follows, and I suspect that these are the words which prod such a statement as "Nothing happens, twice." Gogo says "Nothing to be done" as he tries unsuccessfully to take off his boot. Didi agrees, but he is thinking of his own situation; he can't urinate. But Gogo does pull off his boot a few moments later, immediately after Didi repeats Gogo's opening line, thereby allowing the phrase to become a refrain and allowing us to doubt its truth. And Didi does urinate later, torrentially, with Gogo admiring his offstage performance. In the play's beginning, therefore, we encounter the significant pattern of Beckett's presentation: a statement uttered in a succinct, conclusive way, immediately or later contradicted by deed or word. Here are some obvious examples of the important statement-denial pattern:

VLADIMIR: A ditch! Where?
ESTRAGON: (*without gesture*) Over there.
VLADIMIR: I'm going. (*He does not move.*)
ESTRAGON: I don't know. A willow.
VLADIMIR: He said Saturday. (*Pause.*) I think.
ESTRAGON: What do you say? (*They say nothing.*)
VLADIMIR: I'll give it [the hat] to him. (*He does not move.*)
ESTRAGON: Adieu. Adieu. Adieu. (*No one moves.*)
VLADIMIR: Yes, you know them.
ESTRAGON: No, I don't know them.
VLADIMIR: Don't touch me. Stay with me.
ESTRAGON: Well, shall we go?
VLADIMIR: Yes, let's go. (*They do not move.*)

Gogo validates the pattern in his own inimitable way when he tells Didi: "That's the idea, let's contradict each other." The result of this repetitive pattern of statement-denial is stalemate and uncertainty, which is reinforced, of course, by the play's larger balances and uncertainties: one thief saved, the other damned; one messenger beaten, the other not; the tears of one person transferred to another person; you laugh and it hurts your pubis. And so on. Lucky's speech begins with the words, "On the other hand," and that is where we always seem to be—not least in connection with persons. Beckett is relentless in his strategy of balances, of "on the other hand." Once he sets up his pairs, we are forced to think and feel only in terms of antithesis. Gogo doesn't exist without Didi, Pozzo without Lucky, goat boy without sheep boy, one thief crucified without the other, the waiters without Godot, and conversely Godot without the waiters. Similarly, outside of the play but putting subtextual pressure on it, we feel other pairs that exist only as pairs. Can we think of Laurel without Hardy? Cain without Abel? *King Lear* without the Fool? One of Chaplin's boots without the other? Again and again, Beckett offers a strategy of balances, of antitheses, of stalemate, a strategy which pushes the audience into an atmosphere of precariousness and uncertainty. There's something unbalancing about balances, disquieting about silences. Beckett makes us alert to contradictions, receptive to a dramatic world based on "perhaps."

We return to "Nothing to be done," the assertion which begins the statement-denial pattern, a statement reinforced later when Gogo says, "Nothing happens, nobody comes, nobody goes, it's awful." Anouilh believed that Gogo's words best summarize *Waiting for Godot*. His attitude is close to Mercier's belief that "Nothing happens, twice." But the play's activity answers the play's assertions. Something—more than one thing—happens; somebody—more than one somebody—comes and goes; and it's awful anyway. Many things happen. The play, in fact, is a busy one. If nothing is an important idea in the play—and it's a word that rings out clear in many and different contexts—then the play's business or "busy-ness" deals with much ado about nothing, so much ado, almost a panic of activity at times, that the frozen ends of each act must be effective, which they are. Whether the ado comes to something is an important consideration in any discussion of the play's genre, but first—in the light of all the critical commentary that suggests that nothing happens in the play—it must be established that there is an ado. This is the ado of comedy, it seems. After all, what have we? Two bums in baggy pants, wearing bowlers, waiting around, scrounging for food, trading insults, being beaten, having trouble with boots, switching hats, losing trousers, pratfalls—traditional clowns coming from the music hall or the circus or the movies. Their routines, producing laughter, are clearly happening onstage. The reason their activity seems to be "nothing" is that Beckett prods us to see it in an antithetical context. He sets us up to see these routines as ways to pass the time while waiting for Godot. If Gogo and Didi were not waiting for Godot, their activity would be a series of vaudeville acts, some broadly farcical, which we would applaud for their intrinsic entertainment value. We wouldn't say, "Nothing happens." We hear that "nothing happens," and we can say with Mercier, "Nothing happens, twice" because Beckett forces us to have a specific something in mind. He posits a frame of reference and never allows us to forget it.

"Nobody comes, nobody goes." Not true. Pozzo and Lucky come and go—and what a coming and going! Beckett punctuates their movement with Pozzo's opening and closing word in act 1: "On!" In that act the "On!" is repeated by Pozzo again and again and mimicked by Gogo and Didi. Of course, Beckett, forever working his balances, is allowing Pozzo's "On!" to accentuate the opposite condition of Didi and Gogo. They are on the road, but they are not going on the road. Pozzo and Lucky have direction; Didi and Gogo are tied to a place. The coming back of Pozzo and Lucky in act 2 reveals the results of their movement, one blind and helpless, the other dumb and helpless. Movement has led to devastation, it seems. Pozzo could utter with Winnie of *Happy Days*, "What a curse, mobility." When Pozzo leaves act 2, that is, when he leaves the play, he exclaims his final "On!", and we know—in the light or dark of what he says about birth and death and the night that comes so quickly—we know that his direction is death. In that respect and in the context of the play, perhaps his mobility may not be as much of a curse as Didi's and Gogo's stationary uncertainty about "the last moment."

Not only do Pozzo and Lucky come and go and come and go, but so, too, does the Boy Messenger of Godot. Whether it's the same boy or two different boys, we still have the coming and going. The Boy doesn't have the emphatic movement of Pozzo and Lucky, a movement emphasized not merely by the driving quality of master and whip and by the word "On!" but also by Pozzo's obvious relish in being able to sit down and in Lucky's desire to stop and sleep on his feet. The Boy is tentative; he enters haltingly, but before each act ends, he too exits running. In short, there are comings and goings, which contrast significantly with the staying of Didi and his friend Gogo (how ironic that name sounds!). Only the Godot we are waiting for does not come, and Gogo and Didi cannot go until he comes.

"Nothing to be done," therefore, must always be interpreted with the idea of waiting for Godot in mind. Whatever Didi and Gogo do cannot bring Godot there, and they cannot stop waiting for Godot. They do a lot, but the waiting must persist. Waiting—even that idea seems to belong to the province of comedy. Whatever comedy we witness, we are waiting for the ending, when intrigues will cease, when harmony will be restored, when Jack will get Jill, when the piano will get to the top of the stairs, when the little tramp will walk into the horizon, jauntily swinging his cane. A lot of things happen on the way to the end, but we know—because we are in a world of comedy—that a specific kind of ending will come. It's a closed world that opens at the end to "happily ever after"—and that is the open secret of comedy. However, the waiting here, in *Waiting for Godot*, is uneasy waiting, hopeless waiting, more tragical than comical. It is posited in an antithetical, precarious world, where comic routines try to hide the fact of waiting, but where the dramatist is forever reminding us that we are waiting for Godot. Ah! And because we know that Godot will not come—and if we didn't know it from the play's texture, we certainly know he will not come during the play because he is not listed in the dramatis personae—that predictable sense of closure, that special satisfaction of comedy, is not experienced. Waiting, in Beckett's play, becomes connected with what life is, with the presentness of the moment, even the preciousness of the moment—"I'll never forget this carrot!" And this pushes it toward tragedy even though waiting cannot be thought of as an action in the Aristotelian sense. *Waiting for Godot* has no beginning, middle, and end. It is all middle, twice. But end, I wish to argue, is felt throughout, the balance of comedy and tragedy tilting toward tragedy. It is necessary, in this connection, to confront Beckett's label, tragicomedy, head-on.

It is surprising that Beckett gave a label to his play when he translated it into English. I have found no explanation for this in any of the accounts of his work that I have consulted, and it needs an explanation because we know that Beckett disliked labels. In his essay on Joyce, he said: "The danger is in the neatness of identification." His plays reject a criticism that classifies and defines, that seems definitive. He believed that critics of *Godot* were imposing specific explanations on a play that was trying to avoid definition. Then why did he identify *Waiting for Godot* as a "tragicomedy"? Granted, the term "tragicomedy" is not a neat identification because it carries the weight of an unclear tradition and it seems paradoxical. Its oxymoronic quality must have pleased Beckett, the lover of complementarity and balance, and perhaps Beckett used it so that we should not lodge his play in one generic camp or the other. Perhaps he was trying to protect himself against the neatness of identification associated with either tragedy or comedy. In part, he achieved his purpose, if that was his purpose, because the critics who discuss the balances in his work, including the balance between the tragic and the comic, may have been prodded to do so by the label "tragicomedy." However, because all balances are difficult, because pure complementarity cannot be achieved, many of our best critics have tilted the play toward comedy. Ruby Cohn, for example, calls her fine and influential book on Beckett *The Comic Gamut*, and Hugh Kenner, as another example, discusses Beckett in his book *The Stoic Comedians*. And they may be right because of the rich and various comedy that the play contains and because Beckett's label "tragicomedy," although it does not commit itself to one genre or the other, does tilt its weight toward the noun "comedy," with the adjective "tragi," like most adjectives, having less weight. I assume that Beckett wants us to consider, at least in part, the traditional use of that difficult word. Yeats, for example, said that "Shakespeare is *always* a writer of tragicomedy," and we would agree with him if we considered a tragicomedy to be any play that contains both tragic and comic elements. *The Merchant of Venice* is tragicomedy, containing tragic moments in a comedy, and so is *Hamlet*, containing comic moments in a tragedy. Sir Philip Sidney, in his *Defense of Poesie* (1595), was contemptuous of any attempt to mingle "kings and clowns," labeling such an attempt "mongrel tragicomedy." (If we consider Beckett's autocratic master Pozzo a king of sorts for some—perhaps for Godot himself—then *Waiting for Godot* comes close to Sidney's description.) Of course, Sidney's classical contempt had no effect on the practice of mingling kings and clowns in the English theater, which grew naturally out of the medieval native tradition, where such mingling took place. A working definition of tragicomedy was provided by John Fletcher, who, in his preface to *The Faithful Shepherdess* (1608), said that tragicomedy lacks deaths and therefore is no tragedy, but brings some near it and therefore is no comedy. Here again Beckett's play conforms to type—no one dies, but some are near it. Fletcher's definition goes on to assert that in tragicomedy "a god is as lawful . . . as in tragedy, and mean people as in comedy." This, too, reflects Beckett's play if we wish to consider Godot a god whose presence (or absence) is felt; certainly Didi and Gogo are "mean people." On the other hand and in the spirit of balance, is it not possible that Beckett's is the modern use of that difficult generic term? Beckett may believe, with Ionesco, that in our time the comic is tragic and, therefore, that there is no difference between the comic and the tragic.[1] After all, Beckett has Nell say in *Endgame*, "Nothing is funnier than unhappiness." Beckett may accept Dürrenmatt's belief that "we can achieve the tragic out of comedy. We can bring it forth as a frightening moment, as an abyss that opens suddenly."[2] Here, too, Beckett's play, so rich, open to so many possibilities, can be a clear example of Dürrenmatt's definition. It is Dürrenmatt's definition, I believe, that comes closest to the tone and effect of *Waiting for Godot* because that definition tilts the weight toward the tragic. Beckett places a classification before us, perhaps teasing us (and he is often teasing us) to play with both sides of the oxymoron, perhaps trying to prevent us from committing ourselves to one side or the other. But when a dramatist writes a play that does not provide any screen for his audience to protect itself from a perception of itself, when a dramatist brings us so close to that abyss, when a play elicits the kind of emotions one feels when experiencing traditional tragedies, then Beckett's own balanced classification should be questioned—not an unreasonable thing to do because Beckett seems to want us to question everything. He is always telling us to distrust language, asserting that words "falsify whatever they approach."

I maintain that something happens in *Waiting for Godot*; that the play presents movement of a special kind; and that what happens makes us uneasy, plays with our expectation, elicits questions, prods us to examine what is hidden even as it offers so much that is not hidden, so much that is present, there, in physical stage image. The physical prods the metaphysical, imploring us, it seems, to search for meaning, but at the same time forcing us to distrust meanings because Beckett relentlessly presents balances, antitheses, expectations defeated, certainties questioned, statements contradicted. One such statement, as we have seen, is "Nothing to be done." In one sense, nothing can be done; in another, much is done. Or take the seeming balance of the two acts. Yes, things are happening again, but they are happening more intensely and more speedily—and this is absolutely important when we try to gauge a play's effect on an audience. In *Godot* there is a rush toward the end, one feels, even if the end offers a kind of impasse instead of the conventional closure. The play's movement is more linear than circular. Certainly, Beckett is fond of the circle, and that is what repetition is—a word, a gesture, a movement, an idea, coming back on itself. But his circles are part of the pattern of setting up expectations and modifying them, keeping us ever-alert as an audience, shaping our responses. Take, as an important example, the seemingly circular dog song at the beginning of act 2:

> A dog came in the kitchen
> And stole a crust of bread.
> Then cook up with a ladle
> And beat him till he was dead.
>
> Then all the dogs came running
> And dug the dog a tomb—
> *He stops, broods, resumes*:
> Then all the dogs came running
> And dug the dog a tomb
> And wrote upon the tombstone
> For the eyes of dogs to come:
>
> A dog came in the kitchen
> And stole a crust of bread.
> Then cook up with a ladle
> And beat him till he was dead.
>
> Then all the dogs came running
> And dug the dog a tomb—
> *He stops, broods, resumes*:
> Then all the dogs came running
> And dug the dog a tomb—
> *He stops, broods. Softly.*
> And dug the dog a tomb . . .[3]

We could go on and on with the song, and therefore it is circular and seems never-ending, but Didi's brooding repetition of the word "tomb" "tomb" "tomb" gives that idea a conclusiveness, a finality—the word itself a final destination. The song is circular, but the effect is linear. Interestingly, the dog song—so clear in its syntax, using so simple a vocabulary, so right as a popular round for common folk—the dog song, with its repetition and its emphasis on death, brings to mind Lucky's very different speech of act 1—different because of its incoherence, its obscure allusions, its frenzied delivery, but clear in its repetition of key words, like "on" (Pozzo's word) and "cold" and "dark" and "abode of stones" and clear in its emphasis on death. The dog song ends with "tomb"; Lucky's speech ends with "... the labors abandoned left unfinished graver still abode of stones in a word I resume alas abandoned unfinished the skull the skull in Connemara in spite of the tennis the skull alas the stones Cunard ... tennis ... the stones ... so calm ... Cunard ... unfinished ..." That last word, "unfinished," forces us, because of Beckett's presentation of balance and antithesis throughout the play, to think of finished and more specifically the "It is finished" of Jesus (in one of the four Gospels, a less than reasonable percentage) where the stones and the skull and the dark and the cold have led us. The direction is toward the dark. Only Didi and Gogo and Pozzo and Lucky are not there yet. Jesus' agony is over; perhaps he is more lucky because they crucified more quickly in those days. Lucky's speech is unfinished with the word "unfinished," but the speech does go somewhere and where it goes—that cold, dark, stony abode—is situated closer to the locus of tragedy than comedy. And that is where Pozzo's act 1 speech on the sky also goes. So much attention is paid to Lucky's speech—and rightly so because it seems to touch the identity of Godot—that one tends to ignore Pozzo's important words on the sky and the night, words which come before Lucky's speech. Pozzo is concerned that everyone onstage listen to him, as he looks at the sky. Even Lucky must be jerked out of his somnolence. "Will you look at the sky, pig!" Then Pozzo speaks, with Beckett carefully controlling the pauses and the balance between the lyrical and the prosaic, another kind of antithesis in a play filled with antitheses.

> POZZO: What is there so extraordinary about it? Qua sky? It is pale and luminous like any sky at this hour of the day. (*Pause.*) In these latitudes. (*Pause.*) When the weather is fine. (*Lyrical.*) An hour ago (*he looks at his watch, prosaic*) roughly (*lyrical*) after having poured forth even since (*he hesitates, prosaic*) say ten o'clock in the morning (*lyrical*) tirelessly torrents of red and white light it begins to lose its effulgence, to grow pale (*gesture of the two hands lapsing by stages*) pale, ever a little paler, a little paler until (*dramatic pause, ample gesture of the two hands flung wide apart*) pppfff! finished! it comes to rest. But—(*hand raised in admonition*)—but behind this veil of gentleness and peace night is charging (*vibrantly*) and will burst upon us (*snaps his fingers*) pop! like that! (*his inspiration leaves him*) just when we least expect it. (*Silence. Gloomily.*) That's how it is on this bitch of an earth.

This is followed by a long pause. Pozzo's speech does not contain the terror of Lucky's tirade, lacking its intensity and relentlessness. But the dying of the light, growing paler and paler as Pozzo's hands are flung wider apart, thereby allowing the fading to include all of space, brings us to that word "finished," followed by the idea that night bursts on us "pop! like that!" Pozzo is here predicting exactly what we will see onstage at the end of both acts—the failing light, the moon rising quickly, "in a moment it is night."

In short, whether we are journeying "On" toward skulls or waiting for the light to fade into pale nothingness, we are moving toward the night, and that is the movement of tragedy.

Act 2 seems to repeat act 1, but the Pozzo and Lucky of act 2 are in desperate straits. The passing of time has led them to blindness and dumbness. We know that time has passed because of the appearance of a few leaves on that bare tree. Pozzo is now a pitiful creature—"Help!" is the word he utters repeatedly—and Lucky can no longer dance or talk. They are winding down. Pozzo's last "On!" as he leaves the stage, now closely tied to Lucky, is leading them both to death. That "On!" is itself tied to Pozzo's most important last words:

> POZZO: Have you not done tormenting me with your accursed time! It's abominable! When! When! One day, is that not enough for you, one day he went dumb, one day I went blind, one day we'll go deaf, one day we were born, one day we shall die, the same day, the same second, is that not enough for you? (*Calmer.*) They give birth astride of a grave, the light gleams an instant, then it's night once. more. . . . On!

For Pozzo, everything is happening in an instant, the same day, the same second. A short day's journey into night.

Didi and Gogo are also more desperate in act 2. They seem to be doing the same things, but they are doing them more quickly, more anxiously. They realize, as Didi says, "that things have changed since yesterday." "Everything oozes," says Gogo. That Gogo's anxiety about Godot is greater in act 2 than in act 1 is manifested in his more insistent questioning of Godot's coming and in his many "Ah"s. (Bert Lahr, instinctively sensing Gogo's desperation, claims that he added many more "Ah"s than Beckett provided.) Didi's anxiety is bound up with a higher awareness than that of his friend. In act 2, in contrast to act 1, he tells the Boy messenger that Godot "won't come this evening," that "he'll come to-morrow." He knows. And he recognizes even more than that when the Boy tells him that Godot "does nothing" and has a white beard. Didi's "Christ have mercy on us!" suggests that Lucky's speech about a personal God with a white beard who condemns or saves us "for reasons unknown" got to him. And Didi's generalizing comments on his condition—uttered while Gogo is sleeping, just before the messenger comes, and just after Pozzo and Lucky leave—reveal a new awareness and place him on the same tragic ground as *King Lear*.

> VLADIMIR: Astride of a grave and a difficult birth. Down in the
> hole, lingeringly, the grave-digger puts on the forceps. We have
> time to grow old. The air is full of our cries. (*He listens.*) But
> habit is a great deadener. (*He looks again at Estragon.*) At me
> too someone is saying, he is sleeping, he knows nothing, let him
> sleep on. (*Pause.*) I can't go on! (*Pause.*) What have I said?

Death and birth. Gravedigger and obstetrician. Shovel and forceps. Tomb and
womb. Cries of tormented man and innocent babe. Watchers and watched.
Those awake and those asleep. A series of seeming balances and antitheses,
complementarities, but again the emphasis is on death. Didi's journey is slower
than Pozzo's; the crucial word is "lingeringly." His is a long day's journey into
night—so painful that he says "I can't go on!" Then a pause. A moment's
reflection. Followed by "What have I said?" For here, too, "habit is a great
deadener"—and waiting will continue. Later, near the play's end, Gogo will
say, "I can't go on like this," followed by the wiser Didi's rejoinder, "That's
what you think." If we believe that tragedy dramatizes the struggle of a hero
with necessity and if we modify—because we are living in our time—the
word struggle to include waiting and if we modify the idea of hero to include
all representations of humanity, even clowns at a boundary situation, aware
that they are situated near that abyss and enduring, then surely the balance
of that stalemated phrase "tragicomedy" is tilting toward the tragic. But if
my many "ifs" are not acceptable—and in a world of "perhaps" why should
they be?—then it is to effect, to subjective response, that our discussion must
be directed. That is where I began, trying to recall those moments in that
1956 production, trying to understand how Beckett's dramatic art shaped not
only my experience but also my response to that experience, which was—for
me, at least—not my response toward comedy, but closer to my response to
plays which we call tragedies. Certainly, we should ask ourselves why Jan Kott,
Martin Esslin, Peter Brook, and others have seen fit to make Shakespeare's
tragedies Beckettian. The most notorious *King Lear* of our time, staged by
Peter Brook and starring Paul Scofield, was inspired, the director tells us, by
Beckett. I believe that Brook distorted Shakespeare by relentlessly fitting him
into a Beckettian mold, but there is no question that the instinct behind that
distortion was right. Beckett and Shakespeare, in his tragedies, occupy the
same ground. They posit vulnerable men in a world of cries, questioning and
puzzled men in a world of mystery, unaccommodated men on a bare landscape.
How can anyone who saw Brook's *King Lear* forget that terrible Beckettian
moment when the blind Gloucester, alone on a bare stage, is sitting with legs
crossed, with bleeding eyes staring directly at the audience, while offstage
sounds tell of war and death. But we need not go only to Shakespeare, who
is so large that he can include everyone. America's most important dramatist,

Eugene O'Neill, is most Beckettian not in his one comedy, *Ah, Wilderness!*, but in his darker play *The Iceman Cometh*, where O'Neill's derelicts, like Didi and Gogo, are frozen in their conditions, awaiting a tomorrow that will never come, where Larry Slade is staring at the skull of death, where Godot comes in the person of a salesman bringing death. I have suggested elsewhere that O'Neill's play could be called *Waiting for Hickey*.[4] (It is no mere coincidence, I believe, that the great revival of interest in O'Neill began with the 1956 production of *The Iceman Cometh*, the year Godot came to New York City.) Let me mention one other Beckettian play which elicits a response that is closer to the tragic than the comic, a play whose genre has been disputed by many critics. Chekhov's *The Three Sisters* could be called *Waiting for Moscow*, a title which succinctly describes what's happening or not happening to the three sisters and a title which suggests the play's closeness to Beckett's in its orchestration of effects, its questioning spirit, its balancing of comedy and tragedy, its haunting last image of those three sisters frozen to their condition near a road which others travel but they cannot. Chekhov insisted to Konstantin Stanislavsky that *The Three Sisters* was a happy comedy, and he was disturbed when his own reading of the play to the actors of the Moscow Art Theater produced tears instead of laughter or smiles. However, he labeled the play a "drama," a term that did not commit him to comedy or tragedy, exactly what Beckett's term "tragicomedy" seems to accomplish.[5]

Admittedly, subjective emotional response may not be the most assuring test for genre although Aristotle's idea of catharsis, his tragic pity and fear, continue to find a place in discussions of tragedy. My response to Beckett's play is what my title indicates, tragic pleasure, the pleasure that arises when the terrible truth about life is verified. Beckett, in as pure a fashion as possible, brilliantly using the resources of theater and language, forces us to face the fact of our precarious existence, in which we wait for night to fall, in which we wonder if anyone is watching, in which we resignedly keep a one-sided appointment, in which all the big questions cannot be answered. The feeling of precariousness stems from Beckett's persistent presentation of balances and antitheses, not only in his characterization and in his stage activity, where "nothing happens" leads to much happening, but in his perplexing use of conventional dichotomies, like day and night, awake and sleeping, sight and blindness, saved and damned, speech and dumbness, birth and death, Cain and Abel, and more. These dichotomies often fuse—with death and birth occurring at the same moment, with night coming on suddenly, with a man answering to both Cain and Abel. Beckett is pushing doubt and ambiguity; he is dramatizing the "perhaps" of our lives, the question mark of our existence, an existence that contains much mundane comedy—those comic routines of ordinary daily life—but that also taps deep sources of anguish and frustration.

By showing us man at the boundary situation, confused about place and time, unsure of his relationship with whatever the large force is that controls our lives, if any, and facing darkness with fear and with questions and with some sense of commitment, Beckett in *Waiting for Godot* is evoking the kind of pleasure we derive from *Oedipus Rex* and *Hamlet* and *King Lear* and *Phaedra* and *The Three Sisters* and *The Iceman Cometh*. He forces us to take a closer step to Didi and Gogo because their condition is our condition. That is the step of participation with characters that we find in tragedy as opposed to observation of characters that we find in comedy. On the face of it, it seems difficult to place those clowns, Didi and Gogo, on the same tragic ground as the characters in the plays I mentioned, but that is where they belong, especially Didi, who, at play's end, is awake, has an awareness of what is happening or not happening, who takes up his fate, painful though it is, and goes on. Going on, in the continuously present world of the play, means waiting. Didi and Gogo, as they continue their waiting, watch us as we watch them. The curtain descends on both sets of watchers. The next day the curtain will rise on Gogo's "Nothing to be done," and he and Didi will wait for Godot. We, the watchers of yesterday, will mimic their waiting in our daily lives. It is precisely because Beckett's view of life in *Waiting for Godot* is verified by the lives we live that he takes his place with those other ultimate realists—Shakespeare, Chekhov, O'Neill—whose plays afford tragic pleasure because they allow us to come to terms with what we know, and it is the highest kind of knowledge because it is *felt* knowledge. I believe that is the reason why those stage images of that particular performance back in 1956 remained with me through the years. And surely that must be one of the reasons we celebrate Beckett's potent art today and stand with Cortez's men "Silent, upon a peak in Darien."

NOTES

1. Eugène Ionesco, *Notes and Counter Notes* (New York: Grove Press, 1964), p. 27.

2. Friedrich Dürrenmatt, *The Marriage of Mr. Mississippi and Problems of the Theatre* (New York: Grove Press, 1966), p. 32.

3. Samuel Beckett, *Waiting for Godot* (New York: Grove Press, 1954), p. 37; (London: Faber & Faber, 1956). Subsequent references are to the Grove Press edition.

4. Normand Berlin, *Eugene O'Neill* (New York: Grove Press, 1982), p. 134.

5. I discuss the Beckett–Chekhov connection in *The Secret Cause: A Discussion of Tragedy* (Amherst, Mass.: University of Massachusetts Press, 1981), pp. 109–18.

MICHAEL WORTON

Waiting for Godot *and* Endgame:
Theatre as Text

Beckett once asserted: 'I produce an object. What people make of it is not my concern . . . I'd be quite incapable of writing a critical introduction to my own works.'[1] Furthermore, whenever directors and critics asked for explanations of *Godot*, he both side-stepped their questions and revealed his distrust of any kind of exegesis. Two examples will suffice here. To Alan Schneider's question 'Who or what does Godot mean?', he replied, 'If I knew, I would have said so in the play';[2] when Colin Duckworth suggested that the characters existed in a modern version of Dante's Purgatory, he responded to the 'proofs' offered to him with a dismissive, if generous 'Quite alien to me, but you're welcome.'[3] As is now clearly established, allusions to Dante are present throughout his novels and plays, but Beckett's position remained resolute; he wanted no part in the process of decoding that haunts critical work, preferring to cling to his belief that: 'The key word in my plays is "perhaps".'[4]

Yet he also said about *Endgame* that 'You must realise that Hamm and Clov are Didi and Gogo at a later date, at the end of their lives. . . . Actually they are Suzanne and me.'[5] Here he was referring to his relationship with Suzanne Deschevaux-Dumesnil, whom he finally married in 1961, and to the fact that in the 1950s they found it difficult to stay together and impossible to leave each other. This statement reveals Beckett's ambivalent response to his position as playwright; he initially allows total freedom to directors, actors

From *The Cambridge Companion to Beckett*, pp. 67–87. © Cambridge University Press, 1994.

and critics, but then wishes to correct their interpretations. Although Beckett only once gave an official interview, his many letters and statements to friends and collaborators reveal a wish to control the performance—and therefore the reception—of his plays. His close friend Jean Martin, who played Lucky in the 1953 première of *Godot* at the Théâtre de Babylone in Paris, said of the rehearsals: 'Beckett does not want his actors to act. He wants them to do only what he tells them. When they try to act, he becomes very angry.'[6] What is most interesting is that whenever he directed or was closely involved in the production of his plays, he focused on different aspects. For example, his 1975 production of *Godot* at Berlin's Schiller-Theater pointed up the bleakness of the play, whereas in the 1978 Brooklyn Academy of Music production directed by Walter A. Asmus, who had lengthily discussed the text and production with him, there was much more comic interplay with the audience.

So Beckett's own uncertainty about his 'certain' *perhaps* may give us grounds for more interpretive hope than is usually admitted. What Beckett says outside the texts of his plays is undoubtedly worth considering, but when he comments on either texts or productions, he is just another critic, just as eligible for sceptical examination as any other interpreter. He may well have said to Deirdre Bair that 'the best possible play is one in which there are no actors, only the text. I'm trying to write one',[7] but the use of the word *text* suggests that we should focus on the text itself and not seek to make our interpretations fit with what the dramatist may have said at any particular moment.

Beckett stressed that 'the early success of *Waiting for Godot* was based on a fundamental misunderstanding, critics and public alike insisted on interpreting in allegorical or symbolic terms a play which was striving all the time to avoid definition'.[8] He is undoubtedly right, but as readers, we are bound to interpret his works within a different context from that in which he wrote them. *Ohio Impromptu*, his most sustained dramatic allegory of reading, opens with the Reader saying twice 'Little is left to tell' and closes with his repeated lament 'Nothing is left to tell' (*CSPL*, 285, 288). This final expression of nothingness is, however, an ambiguous recognition of the inevitability of 'nothing', for it comes at the end of a consideration of what 'nothing' is and whether it can even exist. Following the paradoxical logic of Beckett's position as playwright, director and (anti-)critic, each of us has the right to disagree with him—and the 'obligation to express' (*PTD*, 103).

Beckett's first two published plays constitute a crux, a pivotal moment in the development of modern Western theatre. In refusing both the psychological realism of Chekhov, Ibsen and Strindberg and the pure theatricality of the body advocated by Artaud, they stand as significant transitional works as well as major works in themselves. The central problem they pose is what language can and cannot do. Language is no longer presented as a vehicle for direct communication or as a screen through which one can see darkly the psychic movements of a character. Rather it is used in all its grammatical, syntactic and—especially—intertextual force to make the reader/spectator aware of how much we depend on language and of how much we need to be wary of the codifications that language imposes upon us.

Explaining why he turned to theatre, Beckett once wrote: 'When I was working on *Watt*, I felt the need to create for a smaller space, one in which I had some control of where people stood or moved, above all of a certain light. I wrote *Waiting for Godot*.'[9] This desire for control is crucial and determines the shape of Beckett's last theatrical works; the notion that the space created in—and by—the playscript is smaller than that of the novel, however, needs urgent and interrogative attention.

It is undeniable that, having chosen to write in French in order to avoid the temptation of lyricism, Beckett was working with and against the Anglo-Irish theatrical tradition of ironic and comic realism (notably Synge, Wilde, Shaw, Behan). However, his academic studies had led him to a familiarity with the French Symbolist theories of theatre—all of which contest both French Classical notions of determinism and the possibilities of the theatre as a bourgeois art-form. Mallarmé's vision of de-theatricalization and Maeterlinck's dream of a theatre of statues, reflections, sleepwalkers and silence are undoubtedly behind his first plays, but Beckett questions even these theories in order to create his own, new form of anti-theatre.

In the context of twentieth-century theatre, his first plays mark the transition from Modernism with its preoccupation with self-reflection to Post-Modernism with its insistence on pastiche, parody and fragmentation. Instead of following the tradition which demands that a play have an exposition, a climax and a denouement, Beckett's plays have a cyclical structure which might indeed be better described as a diminishing spiral. They present images of entropy in which the world and the people in it are slowly but inexorably running down. In this spiral descending towards a final closure that can never be found in the Beckettian universe, the characters take refuge in repetition, repeating their own actions and words and often those of others—in order to pass the time.[10] Many critics have insisted that Beckett's early plays are constructed on a series of symmetries,[11] pointing to the fact that characters are often organized in pairs, to the importance of dialogue and repetition, and to the concept of the set-design (notably in *Endgame*, with its underlying thematic and visual metaphor of the chessboard). This view is seductive, but is somewhat blind both to the problematics of the psychology of the characters, who exist as individuals and not just as cogs in a theatrical mechanism, and also to the complex web of references within the plays (*intra*textual reference) and of references to other texts (*inter*textual reference). These various references fragment the surface message of the text by sending the reader off on a series of speculations. However, this fragmentation operates (for the reader) as an opening-up of the text and therefore counterbalances the progressive closure of entropy experienced by the characters.

It cannot be denied, of course, that *Godot* and *Endgame* present many of the themes already explored in the novels, all of which centre on the complex problem of how we can cope with being-in-time.

There is the abiding concern with death and dying, but death as an *event* (i.e., actually becoming 'a little heap of bones'; *WFG*, 9) is presented as desired but ultimately impossible, whereas dying as a *process* is shown to be our only sure reality. Beckett's characters are haunted by 'the sin of having been born' (*PTD*, 67), a sin which they can never expiate. Pozzo remarks that '. . . one day we were born, one day we shall die, the same day, the same second. . . . They give birth astride of a grave, the light gleams an instant, then it's night once more' (*WFG*, 89). Death as a final ending, as a final silence, is absent from the plays. The characters must go on waiting for what will never come, declining into old age and the senility which will make of them helpless, dependent— but decrepit—children again, as exemplified by Nagg in *Endgame* who asks plaintively for 'Me pap' (*E*, 15).

We have here an apparent example of the circularity of existence which was proclaimed by the pre-Socratic philosophers (such as Heraclitus and Empedocles) whom Beckett admired, the difference being that the return to childhood in *Endgame* is merely part of the diminishing spiral that will go on and on—to infinity. It is worth pointing out that Beckett originally intended to make *Godot* a three-act play, but finally decided that two acts were enough; and that *Endgame* started as 'a three-legged giraffe' which left him 'in doubt whether to take a leg off or add one on', but which ended up as a one-act play 'more inhuman than *Godot*'.[12] The reason for these decisions is important. Beckett was fascinated by mathematics (hence his love of chess) and especially by the paradoxes that can be made by (mis-)using mathematical principles. He knew that in mathematical theory the passage from 0 to 1 marks a major and real change of state, and that the passage from 1 to 2 implies the possibility of infinity, so two acts were enough to suggest that Vladimir and Estragon, Pozzo and Lucky and the boy, will go on meeting in increasingly reduced physical and mental circumstances but will never not meet again. The same is true of Winnie in *Happy Days* who will never be completely covered by her mound, just as Achilles will never overtake the tortoise in Zeno's famous paradox. We know from our own empirical experience that Achilles would undoubtedly have overtaken the tortoise to whom he has given a head-start, but in many of his works Beckett uses the genre of paradox as a means of reminding us that in metaphysical terms we can never arrive at our chosen destination (death).

The characters are consequently engaged in a perpetual act of waiting. Much has been written about who or what Godot is. My own view is that he is simultaneously whatever we think he is and not what we think he is: he is an *absence*, who can be interpreted at moments as God, death, the lord of the manor, a benefactor, even Pozzo, but Godot has a *function* rather than a *meaning*. He stands for what keeps us chained to and in existence, he is the unknowable that represents hope in an age when there is no hope, he is whatever fiction we want him to be—as long as he justifies our life-as-waiting. Beckett originally thought of calling his play *En attendant* (without *Godot*) in order to deflect the attention of readers and spectators away from this 'non-character' onto the act of waiting. Similarly, he firmly deleted the word 'Wir' from the German translation of the title *Wir warten auf Godot* (*We're Waiting for Godot*), so that audiences would not focus too much upon the individuality—and therefore the difference, the separateness—of Vladimir and Estragon, but would think about how all existence is a waiting.[13]

The title of *Endgame*, with its references to chess, articulates an equally powerful sense of waiting as reality and as a metaphor for infinity. Beckett's own comments are useful here:

> Hamm is a king in this chess game lost from the start. From the start he knows he is making loud senseless moves. That he will make no progress at all with the gaff. Now at the last he makes a few senseless moves as only a bad player would. A good one would have given up long ago. He is only trying to delay the inevitable end. Each of his gestures is one of the last useless moves which put off the end. He is a bad player.[14]

All those who people Beckett's plays attempt to delay the end and are 'bad players', but it is crucial that Hamm is conceived as a king in a chess game. When two kings are left on the board (this is possible *only* when bad players are playing!), they can never end the game but merely engage in an infinite series of movements around the chess-board. So taking Beckett's metaphor logically implies that Clov is a king—as well as a pawn. This inference accords with the fact that their relationship is one of master and slave/servant. Such relationships have fascinated philosophers from Aristotle through Hobbes, Hegel and Nietzsche to the present day, precisely because they are ambiguous; although the master has social superiority, the servant is actually more powerful, since he is more necessary to the master than vice versa. Thus Clov is stronger than Hamm because he makes his existence possible, just as Lucky is stronger than Pozzo because his apparent servility and inadequacy provide the crutch on which Pozzo constantly leans in order to create or, rather, to proclaim, a sense of his authority.

All of Beckett's pairs are bound in friendships that are essentially power-relationships. Above all, each partner needs to know that the other is there: the partners provide proof that they really exist by responding and replying to each other. In this respect, Beckett was much influenced by the contention of the eighteenth-century Irish philosopher, Bishop Berkeley: *Esse est percipi* (To be is to be perceived). This postulate, which informs much Existentialist thinking[15] and which Beckett quotes in *Murphy* and places as the epigraph to *Film*, underpins the anxious desire of his characters to be noticed: 'Vladimir: . . . [Joyous] There you are again' (*WFG* 59); 'Hamm: You loved me once' (*E*, 14). However, Beckett drew from his—highly subjective—reading of Proust a more cynical attitude: 'friendship is a function of [man's] cowardice', and 'Proust situates friendship somewhere between fatigue and ennui' (*PTD*, 63, 64–5). There is certainly the desire to embrace and be embraced (*WFG* 9, 17, 58, 62), yet there is also a realization that friendship is based on the need to give and receive pity (*E*, 28–9).

If our one certain reality is that '. . . we breathe, we change! We lose our hair, our teeth! Our bloom! Our ideals!' (*E*, 16), this truth is very difficult to accept emotionally. The problem is aggravated by the fact that the time is always 'The same as usual' (*E*, 13) and is therefore 'abominable' (*WFG*, 89). In fact, time does not pass in this world; rather, the characters have to find ways of passing the time. One solution adopted by Beckett's characters is mechanical repetition, reenacting situations without perceiving any significance in these repeated actions—somewhat like Pavlov's conditioned dogs who salivate when the bell rings, even when there is no food. The object of these games is not fun but defence against a world they do not and cannot comprehend or accept. In this, they are like the infant playing what Freud calls in *Beyond the Pleasure Principle* the '*Fort/Da* game'. Freud once by chance observed a boy of one-and-a-half playing with a reel of cotton. The child threw the reel over the edge of his cot, uttering a loud, long-drawn-out 'o-o-o-o', which Freud interpreted as the German word *fort* (gone), and then drew it back by the string with a gleeful *da* (there). Freud argues convincingly that by doing this, the child was compensating for the fact that his mother left him against his will (although she would also come back). His oft-repeated game was a means whereby he himself staged the disappearance and return of an object in order to move from a purely passive situation in which he was helpless to a situation in which he could take an active part and thereby (pretend to) master reality.[16] For Freud, this fundamental defensive need to move from the passivity of an experience to the activity of a game is characteristic of much human psychology. It is certainly enacted by all the characters in Beckett's early plays.

Amnesia heightens their anxiety. As Pozzo says, memory is 'defective' (*WFG*, 38). According to Beckett:

the laws of memory are subject to the more general laws of habit. Habit is a compromise effected between the individual and his environment ... the guarantee of a dull inviolability, the lightning-conductor of his existence. Habit is the ballast that chains the dog to his vomit. Breathing is habit. Life is habit. Or rather life is a succession of habits, since the individual is a succession of individuals.... The creation of the world did not take place once and for all time, but takes place every day. (*PTD*, 18–19)

In other words, time indubitably exists as a force of which the characters are aware in that they become increasingly decrepit, but they have no sense of its *continuity*. If each day is like all the others, how can they then know that time is really passing and that an end is nigh? *Godot* is grounded in the promise of an arrival that never occurs, *Endgame* is the promise of a departure that never happens. This would seem to imply that the characters look forward to the future, yet if there is no past, there can be neither present nor future. So in order to be able to project onto an unlocatable—and perhaps non-existent—future, the characters need to *invent* a past for themselves. And this they do by inventing stories. In both plays the past is invariably regarded with nostalgia:

VLADIMIR: Must have been a very fine hat. (*WFG*, 711)

NELL: [*elegiac*] Ah yesterday! (*E*, 18, 20)

HAMM: She [Mother Pegg] was bonny once, like a flower of the field. [*With reminiscent leer.*] And a great one for the men!
CLOV: We too were bonny—once. It's a rare thing not to have been bonny—once. (*E*, 31)

Crucially, the various stories are never really finished—and they are told not only to give the teller a belief that he or she does in fact have a past but, more importantly, to convince a listener that a past, or at least 'their' past, exists. Failure is the inevitable outcome—even the punch-lines of their jokes fail to be properly understood. The reason is that none of these would-be autobiographers can believe in their own tales or even invent plausible accounts. Hamm may redefine his story as 'my chronicle', that is to say, as a factual account (*E*, 40); however, like everyone else, he is striving not to remember his past but to construct it. Vladimir may say ironically to Estragon, 'you should have been a poet' (*WFG*, 12), but both plays articulate a mistrust of the adequacy of subjectivity. This explains Vladimir's violent refusals to listen to Estragon's dream-recitals (*WFG*, 16, 90).

If both subjectivity and narration are suspect, then any and all communication becomes difficult. Beckett repeatedly addresses this problem, but he makes clear in his plays that he believes that full communication is ultimately impossible:

> HAMM: Yesterday! What does that mean? Yesterday!
> CLOV: [*Violently*]. That means that bloody awful day, long ago, before this bloody awful day. I use the words you taught me. If they don't mean anything any more, teach me others. Or let me be silent. (*E*, 32)

Like Vladimir and Estragon, Hamm would like to be a poetic writer and even in his monologues he searches for the right words:

> HAMM: A little poetry. [*Pause.*] You prayed— [*Pause. He corrects himself.*] You CRIED for night; it comes—[*Pause. He corrects himself.*] It FALLS: now cry in darkness. [*Pause.*] Nicely put, that. (*E*, 52)

With no listener (in this case, Clov) the only alternative is to 'speak no more' (*E*, 52–3). Desolation and isolation on Hamm's part, certainly; also an oblique allusion to Iago's last words in *Othello*. This is one of many references to theatre and theatricality throughout the two plays: for instance, Vladimir and Estragon squabble about whether their evening should be compared to the pantomime, the circus or the music-hall (*WFG*, 35), and Hamm speaks of his 'aside', his 'soliloquy' and an 'underplot' (*E*, 49; the last term is a mischievously double reference to the subplot of traditional theatre and to the plots or graves in cemeteries). We may consequently describe Beckett's plays as being metatheatrical, in that they simultaneously *are* and *comment upon* theatre. These texts, both in performance and when read, challenge the traditional contract between play and spectator or reader, since they deny and, indeed, render impossible the need for what Coleridge memorably defines as 'that willing suspension of disbelief for the moment, which constitutes poetic faith'.[17] We are forcibly reminded that we are being confronted by pieces of theatre and so we seek not so much an identification with the characters and their predicaments as an understanding of what the plays mean and why they (can) mean in a new way.

Beckett's great innovation in *Godot* and *Endgame* is both to question the formal structure that playwrights of previous traditions have felt obliged to respect, and to offer a *mimesis* or representation of reality that recognizes and inscribes the formlessness of existence without attempting to make it 'fit' any model. In 1961, Beckett wrote as follows:

What I am saying does not mean that there will henceforth be no form in art. It only means that there will be new form, and that this form will be of such a type that it admits the chaos, and does not try to say that the chaos is really something else. The form and the chaos remain separate. The latter is not reduced to the former. That is why the form itself becomes a preoccupation, because it exists as a problem separate from the material it accommodates. To find a form that accommodates the mess, that is the task of the artist.[18]

Much earlier, he wrote in his essay-dialogue on the painter Bram van Velde that 'to be an artist is to fail, as no other dare fail' (*PTD*, 125), thereby rewriting his first artistic creed: 'There is no communication because there are no vehicles of communication' (*PTD*, 64; see also 103). There was clearly a major shift in his critical and creative position between the 1930s and 1940s and the 1950s when he composed *Godot* and *Endgame* for, although he continued to juxtapose an acute sense of bleakness and nothingness with a desire for 'control', he discovered that the medium of play-writing afforded him greater freedom to make silence communicate.

The pauses in these plays are crucial. They enable Beckett to present: silences of inadequacy, when characters cannot find the words they need; silences of repression, when they are struck dumb by the attitude of their interlocutor or by their sense that they might be breaking a social taboo; and silences of anticipation, when they await the response of the other which will give them a temporary sense of existence. Furthermore, such pauses leave the reader-spectator space and time to explore the blank spaces between the words and thus to intervene creatively—and individually—in the establishment of the play's meaning. This strategy of studding a text with pauses or gaps poses the problem of elitism, but above all it fragments the text, making it a series of discrete speeches and episodes rather than the seamless presentation of a dominant idea. Beckett writes chaos into his highly structured plays not by imposing his own vision but by demanding that they be seen or—especially— read by receivers who realize both that the form is important and that this very form is suspect. One of his most quoted statements, made to Harold Hobson in 1956, is as revelatory in its 'scholarly mistake' as in its affirmation of a love of formal harmony:

I take no sides. I am interested in the shape of ideas even if I do not believe them. There is a wonderful sentence in Augustine. I wish I could remember the Latin. It is even finer in Latin than in English. 'Do not despair; one of the thieves was saved. Do not presume: one of the thieves was damned.' That sentence has a wonderful shape. It is the shape that matters.[19]

The reference is to the debate about one detail of Christ's crucifixion in *Godot* (*WFG*, 12–13), where the 'wonderful shape' is deliberately presented in an amputated and hesitant way. However, it is significant that, while Beckett later said that he thought the sentence was in St. Augustine's *Confessions*, scholars have been unable to find it there—although it has been pointed out that there is a possible origin in a statement in St. Augustine's *Letters*.[20] What is interesting is that, like so many of his characters, Beckett has a 'bad memory' (*PTD*, 29)—or, rather, a memory that, perhaps involuntarily, alters an original sentence in order to give it greater shape than there is in the original. This suggests that, as a playwright, he considers structure to be more important than any 'message' for the communicative functioning of a play.

This does not mean, however, that he is insensitive to the directive or didactic power of many of the texts to which he alludes. Rather, he seeks to show how their very construction is what makes them suspect. In *Godot*, Estragon replies to the question 'Do you remember the Bible?', 'I remember the maps of the Holy Land. Coloured they were. Very pretty' (*WFG*, 12). In other words, the Bible is just another book for Estragon, a book that he can read or merely look at, rather than believing it to be 'Gospel truth'. It is well known that Beckett refused Christian interpretations of his work, as indeed he refused all reductive readings, but Vladimir's commentary on the Gospel accounts of the crucifixion is indicative of the seriousness of Beckett's life-long subversive meditation on the authority of the Bible. Vladimir reminds us that of the four Evangelists who 'were there—or thereabouts' only one (Luke) speaks of a thief being saved, and goes on 'Of the other three two [Mark and John] don't mention any thieves at all and the third [Matthew] says that both of them abused him.' So 'Why believe him [Luke] rather than the others?' (*WFG*, 12–13). This point is central to Beckett's attitude to all writings, be they sacred or secular: why believe any text wholeheartedly? After all, if even the Gospels provide radically different versions of one single event, why trust any chronicle (especially Hamm's)—or any fiction? As Alice and Kenneth Hamilton argue forcefully and provocatively, the playwright repeatedly refers or alludes to the Bible, especially to the New Testament, because it is one text that he knows he cannot trust: 'Beckett does not use Christian "mythology" just because he knows it, but, more particularly, because he is certain it is not true.'[21]

Important and powerful though their themes may be, what makes these plays so interesting is their exploitation of the liberating possibilities of texts that refer within and outside themselves in order to expose the instability of every apparently solid structure. The tree in *Godot* is a marvellous example of how Beckett refuses to allow concrete images to become (mere) symbols. For the 1961 Paris Odeon revival of the play, the sculptor Giacometti designed a tree that was so crucially emblematic that each evening he and later Beckett would come to the theatre before the performance to tweak a twig.[22] The appearance in Act II of four or five leaves has often been interpreted as a sign of optimism, but this interpretation must be unsatisfactory for it neglects (or forgets) that the text constantly denies time as a hopeful movement forward. The tree has no allegorical meaning—but it does have a textual function. It is first evoked (silently!) in Vladimir's thoughts on ending:

> VLADIMIR: [*Musingly.*] The last moment ... [*He meditates.*]
> Hope deferred maketh the something sick, who said that?
> (*WFG*, 10)

While we might initially read this as just one example of Vladimir's amnesiac discourse, its rehearsal of an archaic syntactic formulation suggests that we need to fill in for ourselves the gaps in his memory. Proverbs 13:12 says: 'Hope deferred maketh the heart sick: but when the desire cometh, it is a tree of life.' Not surprisingly, Vladimir forgets the heart (symbol of life and emotion) and the tree (symbol of life and desire). All he can utter is a half-remembered fragment. The intertextual reader, however, completes the sentence—and is consequently alerted to the complexity of *Godot*'s tree(s).

As the play continues, the references to the tree multiply: it is successively a potential gallows-tree (*WFG*, 17, 53, 93); a paradoxical symbol of change and stability (*WFG*, 60); an inadequate hiding-place (*WFG*, 74); the name of a yoga balancing-exercise (*WFG*, 76); a symbol of sorrow (*WFG*, 93). Furthermore, the references to crucifixion and to hanging ironically evoke the New Testament image of Christ hung on a tree—which is the necessary prelude to the Resurrection. And, of course, in Genesis the fruit of the tree of the knowledge of good and evil, while the only fruit forbidden to Adam and Eve, gives them both their humanity and their mortality. The tree thus means so much that it can have no single meaning, and we should remember that Vladimir and Estragon are not sure if it is even a tree, suggesting it might be a bush or a shrub (*WFG*, 14).

In other words, both the denotative and symbolic functions of language are exposed as unstable modes of communication. The many references to the tree are not so much circular as labyrinthine. Wandering in a textual maze with no centre, the reader follows up one reference, establishes a sense, and then comes across another which suggests another sense. The tree is not just 'an arbitrary feature in an arbitrary world',[23] nor is it a symbol of hope. Rather, in its multiplicity, it serves as an indicator of the play's strategies of saying indirectly, and functions as a 'visual' and 'concrete' representation of the essential textuality of the play.

Consider the discussion of the need to talk in Act II:

VLADIMIR: We have our reasons.
ESTRAGON: All the dead voices.
VLADIMIR: They make a noise like wings.
ESTRAGON: Like leaves.
VLADIMIR: Like sand.
ESTRAGON: Like leaves.
  [*Silence.*]
VLADIMIR: They all speak together.
ESTRAGON: Each one to itself.
  [*Silence.*]
VLADIMIR: Rather they whisper.
ESTRAGON: They rustle.
VLADIMIR: They rustle.
  [*Silence.*]
VLADIMIR: What do they say?
ESTRAGON: They talk about their lives.
VLADIMIR: To have lived is not enough for them.
ESTRAGON: They have to talk about it.
VLADIMIR: To be dead is not enough for them.
ESTRAGON: It is not sufficient.
  [*Silence.*]
VLADIMIR: They make a noise like feathers.
ESTRAGON: Like leaves.
VLADIMIR: Like ashes.
ESTRAGON: Like leaves.
  [*Long silence.*] (*WFG*, 62–3)

Critics have compared Beckett's 'dead voices' to Dante's souls in Purgatory. This connection is, *pace* Beckett and his 'indifference' to erudite interpretations, valid and illuminating, for in Canto I of *Purgatory* we find the following exhortation: 'Here let death's poetry arise to life' (line 7). The 'dead voices' and the dead poetry, the *morta poesia*, refer both to the poetry of the *Inferno* and to the souls who in the *Inferno* are dead to God and His grace, yet the canto immediately goes on to invoke Calliope, the muse of heroic or epic poetry, who is asked to perform some act of resurrection. In other words, the allusion to Dante opens up an area of intertextual speculation on (the possibility of) hope. Furthermore, the references to ashes prefigure a central image and theme in *Endgame*. But what is most important here is the inability to find the right words to describe existence: the leaves may also be ashes. While only the signifiers change, the signified is the constant of nothingness, or, more precisely, of indifferentiation. Even if leaves here and the tree throughout the play are privileged, they must be perceived less as objects with an allegorical meaning than as signifiers in a complex web of textual play.

An analogous example is found in *Endgame* where a concrete detail of set design becomes an intratextual signifier. The initial stage directions tell us that there is 'Hanging near the door, its face to the wall, a picture' (*E*, 11). The position of the picture immediately implies a rejection of something in the past (perhaps the image of someone whom one wants to forget, perhaps a troubling scene), but half-way through the play it takes on a new and more powerful meaning when Hamm says:

> I once knew a madman who though the end of the world had come. He was a painter—and engraver. I had a great fondness for him. I used to go and see him, in the asylum. I'd take him by the hand and drag him by the hand to the window. Look! There! All that rising corn! And there! Look! The sails of the herring fleet! ... All that loveliness! [*Pause.*] He'd snatch away his hand and go back into his corner. Appalled. All he had seen was ashes. [*Pause.*] He alone had been spared. [*Pause.*] Forgotten. [*Pause.*] It appears the case is ... was not so ... so unusual. (*E*, 32)

In his own writings on painters, Beckett insists on impotence and failure, as in his 'dialogues' on Tal-Coat, Masson and, especially, Bram van Velde collected in *Proust and Three Dialogues* and later in *Disjecta*. In *Endgame*, he goes further and suggests that, for Hamm, the artist's vision of desolation leads to madness, for in all beauty he sees only ashes. However, we must remember that this is yet another of Hamm's stories and therefore cannot be wholly trusted. Perhaps there was indeed no 'loveliness' at all, perhaps the artist did see correctly, but had to be certified as mad because no society can allow its inhabitants (or its inmates!) to proclaim and represent the greyness, the entropy, the decaying of existence. Art as truth rather than as prettiness must consequently be refused, so the picture is turned to the wall.

This interpretation is consonant with the pessimism which is so often ascribed to Beckett. Yet the picture has a role in the play that goes beyond simple allegory. Clov later replaces the picture with the alarm-clock, while keeping its face to the wall (*E*, 46): the mechanical has replaced the artistic. As Clov says, 'Something is taking its course' (*E*, 17, 26); this implies that our lives are a series of passive repetitions and that we are merely cogs in a machine that is slowly running down. And then finally Clov places the alarm-clock on the lid of Nagg's bin (*E*, 50): the mechanical has been substituted for procreation as it is incarnated by Nagg who is 'Accursed progenitor' and 'Accursed fornicator' (*E*, 15–16).

The point is not the force of any individual idea but that idea follows idea; each proposes something different but also arises from and refers on to another. This form of intratextual reference may be seen as centripetal, as binding the text together, giving it formal coherence—which is not to say that such reference provides a security blanket for readers. Rather it reminds us that all and every text must be read as text and not as direct communication or as authority. Each symbol is not a specifically coded means of communicating, but a call for participation in meditation and speculation.

A further example reinforces this point. *Endgame* opens:

> CLOV: [*Fixed gaze, tonelessly.*] Finished, it's finished, nearly finished, it must be nearly finished. [*Pause.*] Grain upon grain, one by one, and one day, suddenly, there's a heap, a little heap, the impossible heap. (*E*, 12)

Hamm later takes up Clov's words: 'It's finished, we're finished. [*Pause.*] Nearly finished.' (*E*, 35). This is certainly a repetition, but it is significant that Hamm equates 'we' with the 'it' and the 'something' that dominate Clov's discourse; human beings are running down like an unwound clock, like the universe itself. Beginning with a preoccupation with ending, Clov's musing moves swiftly to the evocation of a paradox regarding the impossibility of genuine, logical progress. This philosophical challenge haunts the play, but most readers are unlikely to pick up the reference until Hamm rewrites Clov's speech: 'Moment upon moment, pattering down, like the millet grains of . . . [*he hesitates*] . . . that old Greek, and all life long you wait for that to mount up to a life' (*E*, 45). Most critics have assumed that these are both allusions to Zeno's millet-seed paradox: 'A grain of millet falling makes no sound; how can a bushel therefore make a sound?' In a sense, this paradox could be used to describe the central anxiety in Beckett's world: because 1 = 0, then, mathematically, 1,000 = 0—and yet we do find 'impossible' heaps, so in what can we believe—in 'logic' or in empirical experience? As so often in Beckett's works, though, the reference is more complex than an amnesiac recollection of a text once read, for another paradox and another 'old Greek' are being evoked. One of Zeno's followers, Eubulides of Miletus, established the *sorites* (or heap) paradox in which he proposed that there can be no such thing as a heap of sand, since one grain does not make a heap and adding one grain is never enough to convert a non-heap into a heap. The problem of Beckett's dramatic use of the heap has exercised many critics. Hugh Kenner offers a challenging new avenue to be explored when he proposes another source: 'Sextus Empiricus the Pyrrhonist used just this example [the heap] to show that the simplest words—words like "heap"—were in fact empty of meaning. It is like asking when a play may be said to have had a "run".'[24]

Beckett's fascination with paradoxes is grounded in his conviction that we can (partially) know only ephemeral moments and that, in a world in which there is no God, we consequently seek for 'logical' explanations—which are themselves fictions and manipulations of reality; even the exact science of mathematics becomes another series of texts to be read with suspicion.

The prospect in *Godot* of becoming 'a little heap of bones' becomes a dominant, if problematic, concern in *Endgame*, and then recurs in concrete form in *Happy Days* as the mound in which Winnie is embedded. Unlike her predecessors, Winnie would like to go on living and talking, so Zeno's paradox of Achilles and the tortoise would comfort her in that it suggests that she will never be completely covered. One must, of course, recognize that Beckett is *using* these paradoxes rather than proposing them as creeds or as models for existence. As with the St Augustine allusion, we shall never know whether his discourse is amnesiac or whether the confusion of Zeno, Eubulides and Sextus Empiricus is deliberate.

What is certain is that his writing is highly intertextual and that Beckett is constantly referring not only to ideas but to the ways in which these ideas have been formulated. The plays are saturated with references to the writings of others, as allusion is piled on allusion or parodic quotation. Many are obvious to 'literate' readers, such as Hamm's frenzied cry 'My kingdom for a nightman!' (*E*, 22) which echoes Richard's cry 'A horse! a horse! my kingdom for a horse!' (*Richard III*, V.iv.7). Others are obvious to enthusiasts of 'popular' culture, such as Hamm's angry response to Nagg's demands for his 'pap': 'The old folks at home!' (*E*, 15) which ironically evokes the nostalgia of the well-known American song *Swanee River*. Intertextual references are essentially centrifugal. They fragment the text and send readers off on chases for meaning, for explanation, for enlightenment. Some of these may be wild-goose chases, but in order to understand how Beckett's texts work, we must accept that there is always a *presupposition* of reference. Every Beckett text is built on the premise that whenever we speak or write, we are using someone else's thoughts and language. We are condemned or 'damned' to construct ourselves through the discourses of others, whether we like it or not. And each time we write, we are rewriting and therefore transforming (and deforming!) what we and others previously wrote.

Beckett consistently quotes and repeats himself mischievously throughout his work. He also constantly refers to the writings of thinkers whom he simultaneously admires and wants to challenge. His engagement with pre-Socratic and modern European philosophy is evident in all the plays, and he clearly expects his readers to know—or to be willing to find out about—much mythological figures as Flora, Pomona and Ceres (*E*, 30). The obsession with dying/ending may seem to be the thematic undertow of Beckett's plays; his characters, however, have no sufficient language of their own, and so their discourses are always dependent for meaningfulness on what has already been said—and on the creative intervention of readers.

What Beckett says in his plays is not totally new. However, what he *does* with his saying is radical and provocative; he uses his play-texts to remind (or tell) us that there can be no certainty, no definitive knowledge, and that we need to learn to read in a new way, in a way that gives us space to bring our contestations as well as our knowledge to our reception of the text. Brought up in a severely Protestant environment and having attempted an M.A. dissertation on Descartes, Beckett could not avoid referring to Christian texts and to canonical exegeses. The most obvious and recurring reference is to Descartes's *Cogito ergo sum*. In *Whoroscope* (1930), he aggressively rewrites this founding statement of modernity as *Fallor ergo sum* (I make mistakes, therefore I am). This is a clever and cynical comment on the culturally accepted authority of Descartes and, by extension, of all philosophers. Yet, as the Hamiltons remind us,[25] Descartes's *Cogito* itself echoes St. Augustine's earlier refutation of scepticism *Si fallor, sum* (If I am deceived, I am), and is therefore already engaged in an intertextual manoeuvre. In his plays, Beckett moves from evident manipulative rewriting to indirect reference. In *Endgame*, Descartes's theory is evoked and parodied in terms of emotion when the decrepit Nagg is analysed:

> CLOV: He's crying.
> [*He closes the lid, straightens up.*]
> HAMM: Then he's living. (*E*, 41–2)

The explicit *ergo* ('therefore'/'then') of Cartesian thinking is as true and as false as the implicit 'so ... maybe' of pre-Socratic philosophy; for Beckett's characters and for his readers, logic is the great 'proof', the great temptation, and above all the great lure. Somehow we must persuade ourselves that we exist, somehow we must find justification for our lives. In *Godot* and *Endgame*, as in many of the later plays, such proofs of existence as movement, thinking, dialogue and a relationship with God that have been proposed by philosophers are replaced by anxiety—by an anxiety which leads to the compulsion to repeat and, above all, to fictionalize.

It should be stressed that the fictions and dialogues created by the characters are often based on previous texts. After all, none of us can speak or write unless we have already heard and read. A fascinating feature of Beckett's plays, poems and novels is that, although one can detect a deeply serious meditation on ancient and modern philosophy, he often chooses to use and to parody statements that have become cliches of contemporary thought (Zeno's paradoxes, Descartes's *Cogito*, Berkeley's *Esse est percipi*, and so on). This strategy might seem patronizing, implying both that readers can be expected to recognize only well-known statements, and also that the author knows more and is merely playing a cynical game with his own (low) expectations of readers' knowledge. However, Beckett's intertextual referencing operates more positively. By alluding to, and rewriting, cliches, he is underlining the fact that many statements have become part of common parlance precisely because they say something that is relevant to our individual and communal lives. We are thus propelled into a re-evaluation of why these affirmations have become essential parts of modern thought. In other words, Beckett alerts us to the power of the past and asks that we re-read and reconsider it.

His characters are amnesiac and therefore unaware of what they are (mis-)quoting. Yet they all refer back to the Bible, perhaps because it is the text which both founds our society and poses challenging questions to atheists. On virtually every page of *Godot* and *Endgame*, we find allusions to the Bible and to Christian doxology. While many of these allusions will pass by the 'average' reader/spectator, it is useful to signal some of the ways in which Beckett's plays are informed, and indeed structured, by his Christian education.

We have already seen how, in the Beckettian world, the Gospels should not be trusted as authority. There is undoubtedly, nonetheless, an abiding concern with the Bible—as text and as culturally established authority. While both his parents were Protestants, it was his mother May Beckett who insisted that her children should know the Bible thoroughly. May's Protestantism was stern and canonical and she ensured that her children learned passages by heart. Beckett's adult writerly response, which is grounded in textual familiarity, is essentially atheistic, but it also consists in an exploration and exploitation of the Bible as text—as one text amongst many.

Pozzo describes human beings as 'Of the same species as myself [...] Made in God's image!', and goes on to speak of their likeness to him as 'imperfect' (*WFG*, 23–4). There is here a conscious exploitation by Beckett of the image–likeness opposition established by the writer(s) of Genesis, which sends us back to read the biblical text (Genesis, 1), especially since Estragon later names himself as Adam (*WFG*, 37). Conversely, Hamm says to Clov that humanity might start again from a flea or a crablouse (*E*, 27). Here he is arguing from a mock Darwinian, evolutionist position, but even he cannot refrain from a 'Catch him, for the love of God!' God is omnipresent in Beckett's work as a textual figure who can never be known (because He does not exist or is dead) and who is always present (because the Bible is the founding text of our civilization).

Beckett's plays are full of theological and philosophical questions, such as Estragon's 'Do you think God sees me?' (*WFG*, 76) and Clov's 'Why this farce, day after day?' (*E*, 26), which send us on an exploration of the history of ideas and to an interrogation of authority. It is essential to recognize, with Beckett, that we all remember only fragments of what we once read and that we cannot reconstruct the past: we have parts of the puzzle, but do not see how they could ever have fitted together. When Estragon decides to try Pozzo with other names, Pozzo responds both to Abel and to Cain, thereby representing victim and murderer or 'all humanity' (*WFG*, 83). Yet earlier we find a reference to another pair of brothers when the Boy speaks of his brother who minds the sheep whereas he minds the goats (*WFG*, 51). This might initially appear to be an innocent statement, but as the biblical references multiply, we are drawn back to it and recall that God 'shall set the sheep on his right hand, but the goats on the left' (Matthew, 25: 33). In heaven as on earth, there must always be division and difference; there is no unity, no harmony.

If many of the biblical allusions are semi-occulted, the reader nonetheless senses that there are connections to be made, just as one senses that Lucky's speech must have a logical argument hidden within the incoherence.[26] This sense, is, however, a product of the cultural history that has taught us to seek for meaning, for a cause-and-effect logic. One of the most pungent parodies is Hamm's 'Get out of here and love one another! Lick your neighbour as yourself' (*E*, 44). This patently rewrites Jesus's exhortation 'Thou shalt love thy neighbour as thyself' (Matthew, 19: 19) which is one of the cornerstones of His teaching, yet the phrase occurs also in Leviticus, one of the most censorious books of the Old Testament (Leviticus, 19: 18). If the same divine directive can be given both by the stern avenging God who spoke to Moses and by the compassionate, forgiving Son of God, Jesus, its universal authority is necessarily undermined. This is not to say that Beckett is attacking Christianity, merely that he is reminding us of the textual nature of the Bible and thereby suggesting that it does not have to be believed *in toto* or as dogma.

While the Bible has been used here as an example, the same can be said about all of the many philosophical and literary works to which repeated reference is made. Adorno argues persuasively that Beckett's work is creatively challenging because it can be seen as philosophical satire which uses references to canonical works in order to undermine their authority: he speaks crucially of 'the precariousness of what Beckett refuses to deal with, interpretation'.[27] This view is right, if somewhat unnerving. *Godot* and *Endgame* are powerful (and highly comic) pieces of theatre. They are also works of literature which need to be read as well as seen, which call into play all the knowledge that readers may have. Beckett's vision is frequently described as pessimistic. His works are also said to be elitist in their constant intertextual references: after all, as Estragon says: 'People are bloody ignorant apes' (*WFG*, 13). I would argue that what is crucial is that the *presupposition* of reference, however parodic it may be, is ultimately optimistic—and democratic. None of us needs to notice and follow up every single allusion, yet we cannot but realize that the text of each play is pointing outside itself. Whether our favoured field is the Bible, literature, philosophy or popular songs, we will each pick up some of the references and so accept that all is not even 'nearly finished' (*E*, 12). Our strongest defence against the absurdity and the entropy of existence is the necessity—and the joy—of co-creating the text by continually changing its shape as we connect different ideas and images, as we perceive it to be unauthoritative precisely because it is a *cento*, a patchwork of manipulated quotations.

Suspicious of all authority and especially of the authority of the founding texts of Western culture, Beckett studs *Godot* and *Endgame* with references to these very texts in order to make his readers think and speculate, to make them participate in his anxious oscillation between certainty about what is untrue and uncertainty about what may be true. This abdication of authorial power and this appeal to the creative intervention of readers mark Beckett out as one of the founding fathers of, and one of the major witnesses to, our Post-Modern condition.

Make sense who may (cf. *CSPL*, 316), for make sense we must . . .

NOTES

1. Quoted in Colin Duckworth (ed.), *En Attendant Godot*, xxiv–xxv.

2. See Alan Schneider, 'Waiting for Beckett', in *Beckett at Sixty*, 38.

3. Quoted in Duckworth (ed.), *En Attendant Godot*, lix. Although Beckett's response here insists on his 'alienation' from erudite interpretations, it also prefigures the more generous interpretive stance he adopted in the 1980s.

4. Quoted in Alec Reid, *All I Can Manage*, 11.

5. Quoted in Deirdre Bair, *Samuel Beckett*, 495.

6. Ibid., 449.

7. Ibid., 544.

8. Quoted in Lawrence Graver and Raymond Federman (eds.), *Samuel Beckett: The Critical Heritage*, 10.

9. Quoted in McMillan and Fehsenfeld, *Beckett in the Theatre*, 18.

10. For a particularly illuminating analysis of repetition, see Steven Connor, *Samuel Beckett*, 115–39.

11. See, for example, Hugh Kenner, *A Reader's Guide*, 36.

12. Letters from Beckett to Alan Schneider dated 12 April 1956 and 21 June 1956, quoted in McMillan and Fehsenfeld, *Beckett in the Theatre*, 168.

13. Ibid., 59–60.

14. Quoted in Ruby Cohn, *Back to Beckett*, 152.

15. Although many critics have sought to distance Beckett's work from French Existentialism, Adorno begins his seminal essay on *Endgame* by insisting that 'Beckett's *oeuvre* has several elements in common with Parisian existentialism' (119; I quote from Jones' translation in *New German Critique* which is both more accurate and more subtle than the Weber translation in Chevigny's *Twentieth-Century Interpretations of 'Endgame'*).

16. Sigmund Freud, *Beyond the Pleasure Principle*, in *The Pelican Freud Library*, vol. xi, *On Metapsychology: the Theory of Psychoanalysis* (Harmondsworth: Penguin, 1985), 283–7.

17. Samuel Taylor Coleridge, *Biographia Literaria*, (London: J. M. Dent, 1905), 161.

18. Quoted in Tom F. Driver, 'Beckett by the Madeleine', *Columbia University Forum*, 4. 3 (1961), 23.

19. *Beckett at Sixty*, 34.

20. See McMillan and Fehsenfeld, *Beckett in the Theatre*, 59.

21. Alice and Kenneth Hamilton, *Condemned to Life*, 35–6.

22. See McMillan and Fehsenfeld, *Beckett in the Theatre*, 80.

23. J. P. Little, *Beckett: 'En Attendant Godot' and 'Fin de Partie'*, 57–8.

24. Hugh Kenner, *A Reader's Guide*, 123.

25. Alice and Kenneth Hamilton, *Condemned to Life*, 93.

26. See for instance Anselm Atkins, 'A note on the structure of Lucky's speech', 309.

27. Adorno, 'Trying to understand *Endgame*', 121.

RECOMMENDED READING

Adorno, Theodor W., (trans. Michael T. Jones), 'Trying to understand *Endgame*', *New German Critique*, 26 (Spring–Summer 1982), 119–60.

Alvarez, A., *Beckett*, Glasgow: Fontana/Collins, 1973 (especially chapter 4).

Atkins, Anselm, 'A note on the structure of Lucky's speech', *Modern Drama*, 9.3 (December 1966), 309.

———. 'Lucky's speech in Beckett's *Waiting for Godot*: a punctuated sense-line arrangement', *Educational Theatre Journal*, 19 (1967), 426–32.

Bair, Deirdre, *Samuel Beckett: A Biography*, London: Vintage, 1990.

Beckett at Sixty: A Festschrift, London: Calder and Boyars, 1967.

Bersani, Leo, *Balzac to Beckett*, New York: Oxford University Press, 1970.

Bishop, Tom and Raymond Federman (eds.), *Samuel Beckett*, Paris: Editions de l'Herne, 1976 (see especially the essays by Alan Schneider, Erika Ostrovsky, Julia Kristeva, Walter A. Strauss and Hélène Cixous).

Burkman, Katherine H. (ed.), *Myth and Ritual in the Plays of Samuel Beckett*, London and Toronto: Associated University Presses, 1987 (see especially the essays by Claudia Clausius, Susan Maughlin, Lois More Overbeck and Stephen Watt).

Chevigny, Bell Gale (ed.), *Twentieth-Century Interpretations of 'Endgame'*, Englewood Cliffs, N.J.: Prentice-Hall, 1969.

Cohn, Ruby, *Back to Beckett*, Princeton University Press, 1973.

———. *Just Play: Beckett's Theater*, Princeton University Press, 1980.

———. (ed.), *Casebook on 'Waiting for Godot'*, New York: Grove Press 1967.

———. (ed.), *'Waiting for Godot': A Casebook*, London: Macmillan, 1987.

Connor, Steven, *Samuel Beckett: Repetition, Theory and Text*, Oxford: Basil Blackwell, 1988.

Cousineau, Thomas, *'Waiting for Godot': Form in Movement*, Boston: Twayne, 1990.

Duckworth, Colin (ed.), *Samuel Beckett, En Attendant Godot*, London: Harrap, 1966.

Esslin, Martin (ed.), *Samuel Beckett: A Collection of Critical Essays*, Englewood Cliffs, N.J.: Prentice-Hall, 1965.

Fletcher, John (ed.), *Samuel Beckett, Fin de Partie*, London: Methuen, 1970.

Friedman, Melvin J. (ed.), *Samuel Beckett Now*, University of Chicago Press, 1970.

Graver, Lawrence, *Waiting for Godot*, Cambridge University Press, 1989.

Graver, Lawrence and Raymond Federman (eds.), *Samuel Beckett: The Critical Heritage*, London: Routledge and Kegan Paul, 1979.

Hamilton, Alice and Kenneth, *Condemned to Life: The World of Samuel Beckett*, Grand Rapids, Mich.: William B. Eerdmans, 1976.

Henning, Sylvie Debevec, *Beckett's Critical Complicity: Carnival, Contestation, and Tradition*, Lexington, Ky.: University Press of Kentucky, 1988.

Kalb, Jonathan, *Beckett in Performance*, Cambridge University Press, 1989.

Kenner, Hugh, *A Reader's Guide to Samuel Beckett*, New York: Farrar, Strauss and Giroux, 1973.

Lawley, Paul, 'Symbolic structure and creative obligation in *Endgame*', *Journal of Beckett Studies*, 5 (1979), 45–68.

Little, J. P., *Beckett: 'En Attendant Godot' and 'Fin de Partie'*, (Critical guides to French texts, no. 6), London: Grant and Cutler, 1981.

McMillan, Dougald, and Martha Fehsenfeld, *Beckett in the Theatre: The Author as Practical Playwright and Director*, vol. 1. *From 'Waiting for Godot' to 'Krapp's Last Tape'*, London and New York: John Calder and Riverrun Press, 1988.

Murray, Patrick, *The Tragic Comedian: A Study of Samuel Beckett*, Cork: The Mercier Press, 1970.

Noguchi, Rei, 'Style and strategy in *Endgame*', *Journal of Beckett Studies*, 9 (1984), 101–12.

Pountney, Rosemary, *Theatre of Shadows: Samuel Beckett's Drama 1956–76*, Gerrards Cross: Colin Smythe, 1988.

Reid, Alec, *All I Can Manage, More Than I Could: An Approach to the Plays of Samuel Beckett*, Dublin: Dolmen Press, 1968.

Simard, Rodney, *Postmodern Drama: Contemporary Playwrights in America and Britain*, Lanham, New York and London: University Press of America, 1984.

States, Bert O., *The Shape of Paradox: An Essay on 'Waiting for Godot'*, Berkeley and Los Angeles: University of California Press, 1978.

Velissariou, Aspasia, 'Language in *Waiting for Godot*', *Journal of Beckett Studies*, 8 (1982), 45–58.

Zurbrugg, Nicholas, *Beckett and Proust*, Gerrards Cross: Colin Smythe, 1988.

RUBY COHN

En attendant Godot
(Waiting for Godot)[1]

Beckett did not set out to punctuate his fiction with a play. The holograph of his play shows much less revision than do manuscripts of his novels. In a cheap graph paper notebook Beckett's execrable handwriting runs across the recto pages, then doubles back to the book's beginning to continue on the verso pages. Only occasional crossouts and a relatively small quantity of doodles connote impediments to the creative flow. The general impression is of almost continuous writing, and indeed the play, begun on October 9, 1948, was completed on January 29, 1949. At no point in the manuscript is there a scenic breakdown, as in the aborted *Human Wishes*; nor do we find a cast of characters, as in *Eleutheria*. The improvisatory quality of the play seems to have emanated from Beckett's own quasi-improvisatory composition—at least initially.

The manuscript opens on the bare setting: "Route à la campagne, aver arbre" [A country road, with tree]—themselves horizontal and vertical coordinates on the graph page. There follows a scenic direction about a nameless "vieillard" trying to take off his shoe. Another "vieillard, ressemblant au premier" then enters. The first old man, attacking his shoe again, then speaks what was to become the most celebrated opening line in modern drama: "Rien a faire" [Nothing to be done]. The second old man, moving forward with comic spavined gait, expands "Rien à faire" to the human condition, however he may struggle against its

From *A Beckett Canon*, pp. 176–183, 399. © University of Michigan, 2001.

fatalism, "songeant au combat" [musing on the struggle]. Addressing himself as Vladimir, the second old man effectively names himself, and immediately afterwards in the manuscript occurs Beckett's name for the first old man— Lévy—and so he remains throughout the first act of the manuscript. Early in act 2 Beckett suddenly changed Lévy's name to Estragon, but that name enters the dialogue only late in the manuscript, in Vladimir's soliloquy.

When Pozzo and Lucky first enter, they are designated as a large man and a small one; they are seen in comic contrast before they are named. Pozzo announces his name almost at once, but the name Lucky is first attached (by Pozzo) to the rightful recipient of the discarded chicken-bones. The broadly European flavor of the four names—Slavic Vladimir (meaning prince of peace), French Estragon (a bitter herb of Arabic origin), Italian Pozzo (meaning a well), and the ironic English Lucky—emerged during composition, as did the alternate names for the friends—Didi and M. Albert for Vladimir, Gogo, Macgrégor, and Catulle for Estragon. In Beckett's French fiction female names were variable, but *Godot* extends that indeterminacy to the two men who meet each evening to keep their appointment. Although Pozzo's name is stable, it resembles Godot sonically.

The manuscript of *En attendant Godot* differs in many small details from the version published by Les Editions de Minuit in 1951, some three months before the Paris premiere. However, formal symmetries are present from the start—especially the unparalleled repetition of the first act by the second: at twilight two friends meet by a tree to wait for Godot; a landowner and his knook dally with them and then depart. A boy messenger announces that Godot will not come tonight but surely tomorrow. Upon the boy's exit, night falls swiftly, and the moon rises. Finally one friend suggests that the couple leave, but they do not move.

Because of its very bareness, the plot is fertile ground for a variety of subjects, and the second act echoes the first in such disjunctive topics as food, the tree, bones, the sky, time, place, memory, pain or discomfort, suicide, offstage beating of Estragon, Vladimir's onstage welcome of Estragon, Vladimir's refusal to listen to Estragon's dreams, and the friends' sporadic nostalgia for the past that contrasts with their uncertainty about the future. The variety is camouflaged under the sprinkling of *encores* that underline the repetitiousness of word and deed.

Vaudeville turns erupt from the start. *Godot* opens with a hoary clown number: Estragon struggles to take off a tight shoe, and during the course of the play it is he who is familiarly funny. He begins a bawdy joke, speaks in baby talk or in a foreign accent or with full mouth; he delivers the two-lung number, dangles a phallic carrot, mimics Lucky as a beast of burden, tries to hide behind a frail tree, and finally drops his trousers. Despite Vladimir's superior sophistication, he buttons his fly, laughs painfully, spits disgustedly, pulls miscellaneous objects from his pockets, imitates Lucky, and minces like a mannequin. Together Vladimir and Estragon juggle three hats, take gorilla postures, huddle in exaggerated fright, examine Lucky as an object, pose as scouts on the lookout, "do" the tree, tug at a rope that nearly knocks them down when it breaks. They manipulate their respective props—Vladimir his hat and Estragon his shoe—precisely and identically. Their nicknames Didi and Gogo are comically endearing, and their scenes of cross-talk establish the dominant dialogue rhythm of the play.

In contrast to the vaudeville of Vladimir and Estragon, Pozzo and Lucky are more erratically comic. Pozzo is ridiculous in his self-inflation. Although it is Estragon who mistakes him for Godot, Pozzo twice plays variations on that enigmatic name, but he invokes a genuine deity when he examines his new acquaintances: "De la même espèce que Pozzo! D'origine divine!" [Of the same species as Pozzo! Made in God's image!] A self-conscious performer in act 1, Pozzo sprays his throat ostentatiously, demands undivided attention for his recitation, alternates between lyrical and prosaic tones, and anxiously solicits the reactions of the two friends. Like comics of the vaudeville tradition, Pozzo misplaces his props—pipe, atomizer, and watch. It is when Pozzo boastfully contrasts himself with Lucky that the two remove their bowler hats, and Beckett first notes that all four men wear "chapeau melon" [bowler hats]. We scarcely need Pozzo to point out the contrast between himself and his rarely comic "knook"; yet the object of scrutiny hovers on the comic in the elusive question of why he doesn't put down his bags (and Pozzo's preposterous answer). When Pozzo offers Lucky's performance to the two friends, the knook at first confuses thinking with dancing. Lucky's "think," often performed as a farcical turn, is the bravura piece of the play. Beckett's manuscript reveals little difficulty in its composition, written in a single block on several pages, without the three-part division to which the author later called attention—indifferent deity, dwindling humanity, and stone-cold universe. (In revision, Beckett "vaguened" Lucky's "think" through increased sound play, repetition, and incoherence.) After silence is imposed upon Lucky, the act 1 comedy ebbs toward an end.

In act 2 Vladimir again seeks to fill time, and he is grateful for reinforcements in the return of Pozzo and Lucky. After their reentrance (from the opposite wing, although neither manuscript nor printed versions designates it), the four adult characters take comic pratfalls. That late in the play the characters have already established themselves as performers, physically and verbally—the friends in their duets, but Pozzo and Lucky in their center-stage recitations. Even the day itself has, according to Vladimir, come to the end of its repertoire.

Repertoire it is. Resolutely *ill* made dramatically, *En attendant Godot* seeks to conceal the depth below the farce, but the tragicomic blend has appealed to imaginations throughout "this bitch of an earth." In one way or another, audiences have recognized themselves as waiting, whether in schools, prisons, theaters, or even country roads. So the overarching action of *En attendant Godot* was both new and familiar, or familiar in its novelty. As is the very setting of road and tree, each a metaphor for human life. The bare stage, thin plot, and crepuscular light hint at ghosts of cultural traditions, where each culture has recognized its own.

Although Beckett himself has pleaded that *En attendant Godot* seeks to avoid definition, he has larded it with biblical shards, starting with the neologism God-ot. Elsewhere we stumble on the two thieves, whose iconography on either side of Christ is echoed in act 1 when the friends support Lucky, and in act 2 when they support Pozzo.[2] That slave driver is not only made in God's image, but he answers to both Cain and Abel; as Estragon notes: "C'est toute l'humanité!" [He's all humanity]—both victimizer and victim. Passing phrases of *Godot* whisper about the wind in the reeds and the sheep versus the goats from Matthew, and the unanswered cries for help may reflect mordantly upon the parable of the good Samaritan. Vladimir sententiously assigns every man to his little cross, and Estragon avers that he has always compared himself to Christ. Beckett teases us with fragments of a faith that do not cohere (and they are more numerous in English, the Language in which Beckett was taught his Christianity).

Even more insistent than the Bible is the aura of mortality. The many versions of the question about Lucky putting down his bags may be applied to all humanity with its burdens. Linked obliquely to that burden is the shadow of death, however it is dissipated by farce. Early in the play Vladimir expands "Rien à faire" to the suicide that the two friends might have committed in style, jumping from the Eiffel Tower. When suicide shifts to hanging, its gravity is undercut by the anticipation of an erection. Even Estragon's recollection of Vladimir rescuing him from the river (Durance in French, Rhone in English) is squelched by that same Vladimir. At the end of the play the friends' halfhearted attempt at hanging breaks with the fragile cord, but it is vital that Estragon's trousers fall, to sustain the tragi*comic* flavor of suicide.

Suicide is not the only deathly presence in the play. Estragon is confused as to whether the Savior saves the good thief from hell or death. Vladimir warns his friend that, without him, Estragon would be a little heap of bones. We are thus subliminally prepared when Pozzo gnaws at bones, and Estragon gnaws at the gnawed bones. By act 2, we see no bones, but death is present in Vladimir's dog song, which stops each time he reaches the line about burial. When we later hear about bones, they imply the death of civilizations:

VLADIMIR: Ce qui est terrible, c'est d'avoir pensé.
ESTRAGON: Mais cela nous est-il jamais arrivé?

VLADIMIR: D'où viennent tous ces cadavres?
ESTRAGON: Ces ossements.

[VLADIMIR: What is terrible is to *have* thought.
ESTRAGON: But did that ever happen to us?
VLADIMIR: Where are all these corpses from?
ESTRAGON: These skeletons.]

A charnel house is the repository of the "more things in heaven and earth . . . than are dreamt of in your philosophy" but are hinted in *Godot*.

On that twilight scene the most frequent scenic directions are "Un temps" (pause) and "Silence," but their invasive force camouflages Beckett's impressive verbal range—colloquial, austere, formal, interrogative, plangent, vituperative, imaged, abstract. The repetitions—particularly the eight refrains of "waiting for Godot"—establish a groundwork of monotony, but from them blossom clichés, puns, synonyms, rhymes, as well as the friends' verbal games of making conversation, questioning each other, contradicting each other, abusing each other. Early in the play a single stressed word highlights language; Vladimir describes his confused feeling: "Soulagé et en même temps . . . *il cherche* . . . épouvanté. *Avec emphase.* E-pou-van-té" [Relieved and at the same time . . . *he searches for the word* . . . appalled. *With emphasis.* Appalled].[3] Soon afterward Vladimir seeks the antonym of *sauvé* for the bad thief. Much later he hesitates before declaring that he and his friend are "hommes." Although *En attendant Godot* abounds in pregnant monosyllables like these, it also displays polysyllabic comic catalogs—Pozzo's series of Lucky's dances, Lucky's list of sports, the several synonyms for Pozzo's pipe. In the friends' delicate duets about dead voices Vladimir seeks new sounds, whereas Estragon stalwartly repeats his first metaphor.

Beckett's stage musicality is now a critical cliché, so it is perhaps time to return to the human meaning of the tragicomedy. Beckett himself, in preparing the play for performance, noted the twenty-one cries for help, with fourteen ignored. The first meaningful repetition in the play is "Tu as mal? . . . Mal! Il me demande si j'ai mal!" [It hurts? . . . Hurts! He wants to know if it hurts!]. Before the end of the play, we know that it hurts, and we know that we hurt. Many other phrases have taken on extensible significance, outside of the immediate context of the play, from "Rien a faire" [Nothing to be done] to "Elle ne vaut rien" [Not worth a curse] and including "Pour jeter le doute, à toi le pompon" [Nothing is certain when you're about], "Il y a une chance sur deux. Ou presque" [There's an even chance. Or nearly], "Ce n'est pas folichon" [I've been better entertained], "Ça a fait passer le temps" [That passed the time], "On trouve toujours quelque chose . . . pour nous donner l'impression d'exister" [We always find something . . . to give us the impression we exist], "Je ne veux plus respirer" [I'm tired breathing].

Vladimir's last soliloquy subsumes the dreamlike aspect of the friends' existence, the painful indeterminacy of their situation, their problematic interdependence, their objectification in the gaze of unknown others, and he whimpers: "Je ne peux pas continuer. (*Un temps.*) Qu'est-ce que j'ai dit?" [I can't go on! (*Pause.*) What have I said?]. Is he questioning the immediately previous sentence or the whole speech, with its rewording of Pozzo's memorable image: "A cheval sur une tombe et une naissance difficile. Du fond du trou, rêveusement, le fossoyeur applique ses fers" [Astride of a grave and a difficult birth. Down in the hole, lingeringly, the grave-digger puts on the forceps]? Malone was unable to sustain the spirit of play in his fiction, and Beckett diminishes play as the tragicomedy *En attendant Godot* ebbs to an end—this evening.

Soon after Beckett's return to postwar Paris, he was befriended by Georges Duthuit, who had bought from Eugene Jolas the title of the prewar *Transition*, but he changed the "mantic" orientation of the periodical toward art criticism. Duthuit contributed not only to Beckett's social life but also to his precarious material subsistence, commissioning many translations, which Beckett usually chose not to sign. Yet *Three Dialogues* is not a commission, but a distillation of the many art-critical conversations of the two men, Beckett told Federman and Fletcher that the dialogues "merely reflect, very freely, the many conversations we had at that time about painters and painting" (24). To Martin Esslin's query as to whether Beckett wrote down actual discussions with Duthuit, the author replied, "Up," in the humorous tone of the dialogues themselves. Nevertheless, the dialogues were printed in *Transition* as coauthored "by Samuel Beckett and Georges Duthuit," and perhaps Beckett scholars (including myself) have too easily ignored the contribution of Duthuit. I find it surprising that the dialogues have not been professionally performed (so far as I know). Written in English for publication in *Transition*, *Three Dialogues* shows Beckett's shaping eye (and ironic wit) at work even in art criticism.

THREE DIALOGUES by SAMUEL BECKETT AND GEORGES DUTHUIT[4]

Three because the initialized discussants B and D focus on three painters— Pierre Tal Coat, André Masson, and Bram van Velde. The dehiscence of the subject–object relation is the thread (and the standard) of B's critique, although "object" is sometimes "occasion" and once "aliment." In the three-scene sketch the two speakers, B and D, articulate their thoughts in the superior, quasi-hermetic phrasing of Beckett's reviews of the 1930s. B opens each of the three scenes; in the face of D's admiration of Tal Coat or Masson, B presents his view of an art of failure, which is an art beyond art. Each scene concludes with B's defeat, but not before he delivers sentences that critics would subsequently apply to Beckett's own work.

In the first dialogue B derides Tal Coat for merely playing variations upon the old traditional relation between the perceiving artist and the perceived object. It is in reaction against "the Franciscan orgies of Tal Coat" that B enunciates his credo of an art of the nonfeasible: "The expression that there is nothing to express, nothing with which to express, nothing from which to express, no power to express, no desire to express, together with the obligation to express" (*Disjecta*, 139). The Wattesque series of negatives are opposed by the (mysterious) obligation to express.

The second dialogue is more problematic to B, since D's Masson (aided by quotations from the painter) recognizes a crisis in the subject-object relationship, and yet he cannot paint the void. D appreciates what Masson *can* paint, causing B to exit, weeping.

By the third dialogue, D is impatient with B, demanding an explanation of his view of van Velde's "art of a new order," which eliminates "occasion, in every shape and form, ideal as well as material." D then cannily suggests that that very elimination, van Velde's predicament, becomes a new occasion, and he thereby forces B to correct his earlier phrase for Bram van Velde as a painter of predicament (presumably referring to his *Peintres de l'empêchement*). In provoking B to a "connected statement," D admonishes him: "Try and bear in mind that the subject under discussion is not yourself" (144), which suggests to the reader that that is indeed the subject. B's longest speech contains an old Beckett theme: "But if the occasion appears as an unstable term of relation, the artist, who is the other term, is hardly less so." The new rendition of that old theme is, however, more extreme and dogmatic than heretofore; it leads to the inevitable failure of the artist: "to be an artist is to fail, as no other dare fail, that failure is his world and the shrink from it desertion, art and craft, good housekeeping, living" (145). This often quoted espousal of artistic failure must, however, be situated in the context of the anxious relation between subject and object, without converting that relation into a new occasion for art.

Three Dialogues, like Lucky's speech, concludes without conclusion. B seems to elevate van Velde's painting above art. When D requests the second part of B's argument, he, "Remembering, warmly," admits that he is mistaken, but B has been so discursive in his argument that it is impossible to locate the mistake. What is unmistakable is the unstable aesthetic that links B's van Velde with the crisis in Beckett's own fiction, where the occasion, and even the subject, gradually dissolves into the writing process of the protagonists, Molloy, Moran, and Malone.

Notes

1. The holograph of *En attendant Godot* is contained in a single notebook, dated October 9, 1948, on the first page, and January 29, 1949, on the last. Beckett kept it in his possession (but not in his home) to the time of his death. A photocopy was made available to (selected) scholars by Les Editions de Minuit. Excerpts of *Godot* were taped for *Le Club d'Essai* on February 6, 1952, and broadcast on February 17. The play was originally published by Minuit in October 1952, before the stage premiere on January 5, 1953, and during rehearsals Beckett made minor changes in his prompt copy, now at TCD. Beckett's translation into English was first published by Grove in 1954 and by Faber in 1956. There are so many editions of *Godot* that I forgo page references.

2. Beckett traced the arbitrary salvation-damnation of the thieves to a passage in Augustine, which he quoted to Harold Hobson, the English critic: "Do not despair, one of the thieves was saved. Do not presume, one of the thieves was damned." However, no one has been able to find that sentence in the works of Augustine. C. J. Ackerley convincingly argues that Beckett drew it from Robert Greene's "The Repentance of Robert Greene," which ends: "To this doth that golden sentence of S. Augustine allude, which hee speaketh of the theefe, hanging on the Crosse. *There was* (saith hee) *one theef saved and no more, therefore presume not; and there was one saved, and therefore despaire not*" (1998, 213.2).

3. The French *pou*, or louse, causes Vladimir to reexamine his hat for a foreign body. This pun is lost in English translation, but the new pun on "pall" enhances the death imagery. Much later, when they speak of being bound—*lié* in French—Vladimir does not "fait la liaison" phonetically between *pas* and *encore*; this subtle soundplay is lost in translation.

4. First published in *Transition Forty-Nine* (December 1949), under the joint authorship of Samuel Beckett and Georges Duthuit, the *Three Dialogues* are annotated confusingly in Federman and Fletcher (24). Beckett translated part of the third dialogue into French, for a Bram van Velde exhibition in 1957. The full text of that dialogue appeared in *Georges Duthuit*, 1976. *Trois Dialogues* was published by Minuit only in 1998, with the first two dialogues translated by Edith Fournier, *Masson* for the first time and *Tal Coat* reprinted from a 1996 catalog in Aix. I inadvertently (but inexcusably) dropped Duthuit's name in the reprinting of the three dialogues in *Disjecta*, to which my page numbers refer.

CHRISTOPHER DEVENNEY

What Remains?

For it's the end gives meaning to the words.
　　　　　　　　　　—Samuel Beckett, *Texts for Nothing*

We always find something, eh Didi, to give us the impression we exist?
　　　　　　　　　　—Samuel Beckett, *Waiting for Godot*

It is true that one of the greatest difficulties involved in approaching the writings of Samuel Beckett arises from the repeated assaults his texts enact upon themselves, upon their own progress and self-generation, and thus also upon the contexts and resources of traditional literature. The storyteller's art is not Beckett's, and to the extent that his early writings—including the novels *Murphy* and *Watt*, and then later the first-person monologues of *Molloy* and *Malone Dies*, and to a lesser extent *The Unnamable*—unfold around various masks and faces, characters, narratives (of a sort), and plots it is only as a preliminary step intended ultimately to dispel precisely these. But for what? Toward what end? Because they have run their course, and exist now at best as relics of a cultural, artistic, and philosophic ethos of a false humanity. Because now, after the texts of Nietzsche and Wittgenstein, not to mention Proust and Woolf, how can we continue to speak seriously of a stable self, a fixed and inert stratum of *res cogitans* that somehow grounds and stabilizes both the self and the world from a place apart from the movements and instances

From *Engagement and Indifference: Beckett and the Political,* pp. 139–160. © State University of New York, 2001.

of language and grammar? Or, in more literary terms, isn't it clear by now that there are only slight differences between what is referred to as literary character and the Cartesian *ego cogito ergo sum*?

From the very beginning of Beckett's career as a writer, long before the stories or the novels of the trilogy were begun, it was clear that it would be impossible to simply continue in the vein of English (and Irish) letters already set forth. In a letter written in German to Axel Kaun in 1937 and published in 1983 as "The German Letter of 1937" he asserted:

> it is indeed becoming more and more difficult, even senseless, for me to write an official English. And more and more my own language appears to me like a veil that must be torn apart in order to get at the things (or the Nothingness) behind it. Grammar and style. To me they seem to have become as irrelevant as a Victorian bathing suit or the imperturbability of a true gentleman.... Is there any reason why that terrible materiality of the word surface should not be capable of being dissolved?[1]

There are a number of questions raised here; for instance, what exactly would constitute an "official English" for an Irish writer such as Beckett? What is the veil that his own language—whatever that is—appears as which "must be torn apart"? What does it conceal? Despite the appearance of a program of an "assault against words," as it is said elsewhere in the letter, and the tearing asunder of the "veil" of language, phrases that intimate a certain program of writing outwardly sympathetic to the various assaults mounted by avant-garde writers of the early twentieth-century, the references to "grammar and style"—"to me they seem to have become as irrelevant as a Victorian bathing suit or the imperturbability of a true gentleman"—reflect a different direction. Initially, the references to grammar and style indicate an unmistakable impulse on Beckett's part to distance himself from the practitioners of what he had referred to in his essay on Joyce ten years earlier as the "architects of literary stylistics"—in other words, the forebears of the literary styles that make up, and continue the progress of literary culture in the British and Irish contexts. Undoubtedly he has Joyce in mind, but also writers such as Keats, or Tennyson, Swift, Sterne, Coleridge, and so on. In the late 1960s Beckett commented to the critic Richard Coe that he was afraid of English: "you couldn't help writing poetry in it."[2] Marjorie Perloff adds that "this is not ... a facetious remark ... English for Beckett is, after all the language of his childhood, more specifically, the canonical language of 'English literature' as taught to a school boy at the Portora Royal School" where he would undoubtedly have been indoctrinated into the long and weighty stream of British tradition from Shakespeare and Milton, to Keats, Tennyson, and Arnold.[3]

But it was not just from the English style that Beckett sought refuge, but rather style in general, in any guise or form. "Let us hope the time will come," he states in the letter, "thank God that in certain circles it has already come, when language is most efficiently used where it is most efficiently misused." What is meant here by misuse, though, is left purposely ambiguous; apart from declaring that "with such a program ... the latest work of Joyce has nothing whatsoever to do" his only reference is to Stein: "perhaps the logographs of Gertrude Stein are nearer to what I have in mind. At least the texture of language has become porous" (D, 172). But with Stein, at least in Beckett's view, the endeavor has unfolded by accident; she remains, he claims, "in love with her vehicle." Strangely, though, as Beckett offers no examples of what he means by "misuse," the efficient misuse of language that he refers to seems to have a double meaning; on the one hand "misuse" may in fact be language's so-termed correct usage according to grammatical and conventional strictures; while on the other hand, and more typically, the efficient use of language as its "misuse" appears to be meant as a conscious disarticulation of correct usage that he, along with a select number of other writers, has begun to enact in his writing. In either case, inasmuch as style is always to one degree or another a mode or form of accommodation, even consolation that completes, however artificially, the distance that separates a consciousness from the world of things and experience, it is something that must be avoided. Though it may be a departure from realist conventions and more traditional practices of the novel, the religion of style as practiced by a Flaubert—"I value style first and above all, and then Truth"[4]—is to be resisted as much as any other, whether that be the word-apotheosis of a Joyce, or the logographs of a Stein.

But Beckett appears to go even farther than this: "As we cannot eliminate language all at once," he adds, "we should at least leave nothing undone that might contribute to its falling into disrepute. To bore one hole after another in it, until what lurks behind—be it something or nothing—begins to seep through. I cannot imagine a higher goal for a writer today" (D, 172). This goal, which Beckett views as the highest goal for a writer today, is meant in the most extreme sense; ultimately, it is aimed not simply against the strictures and conventions of literary or ordinary language. In the letter Beckett asks Kaun if he minds his errors in German, and then says "from time to time I have the consolation ... of sinning willy-nilly against a foreign language, as I should love to do with full knowledge and intent against *my own*—and as I shall do" (D, 173). Again, though, what Beckett means by "my own" language remains unclear. Conventionally, it would mean his own English. But the fact that Beckett ultimately opted to write in French, only later rewriting his texts in English, suggests that what he has in mind is a full-scale assault not only against English but also against *his own* language, against that language wherein the integrity of a (or *the*) self is at once established and maintained. It is to be an assault against what Beckett termed in his monograph on Proust in 1931 "the great deadening of habit."[5]

Habit, like style, is what sutures a kind of tenuous rapport with the world as it is given in language through the tonality and grace of speech, rhyme, and meter. Style in general, styles of expression, styles of speech are all indexes of habit, of habituation, and habitation, which underwrites the very habits of thought, of speaking, of writing, and of reading within which we live and dwell. These are what must be broken. Though Beckett's point, however discretely, goes farther than this to challenge not only our adherence to a certain aesthetic sensibility, but to challenge our continued cleaving to stable forms of life, to the forms of language that affirm the given and presumed order of reality and being, to the oft-termed real existing conditions that habit perpetuates. Before what Beckett termed "the perpetuum" of reality, human beings enact and reenact according to the changeability of existence and subjects certain orderings of the world. These orderings, though, are first and foremost orderings both of and in language. It is not a matter or question of specific impositions—rightly or wrongly imposed—but rather the habit of imposition as such. It is these habits of expression, habits of thought, of speaking, of reading, and writing that Beckett's writing seeks to unsettle. And it would appear, too, that he has in mind his own habits of expression as much as anyone else's. "Habit," Beckett wrote, "is a compromise effected between the individual and his environment." It is the "guarantee of a dull inviolability. . . . Habit is the ballast that chains the dog to his vomit. Breathing is habit. Life is habit" (pp. 18–19).

* * *

It would take Beckett ten years to fully arrive at what was necessary to begin the dissolution of the "terrible materiality of the word surface." This process is what was undertaken in the late 1940s in the turn to French and the writing in quick succession of the texts of the trilogy—*Molloy, Malone meurt,* and *L'Innomable*—as well as the plays *Waiting for Godot* and *Endgame,* and the earlier stories.

Concerning these texts and this period in his work, in the only formal interview he ever gave during his lifetime, Beckett remarked that:

> At the end of my work (*Á la fin de mon oeuvre*) there's nothing but dust—the namable. In the last book—*L'Innommable*—there's complete disintegration. No "I," no "have," no "being." No nominative, no accusative, no verb. There's no way to go on.[6]

Beckett's remark is a wry illustration of the very circumstance he's describing. He refers to the "end of my work" and then comments, "In the last book—*L'Innomable*—there's complete disintegration"; this would seem to be the end of the matter, but it's not. He continues on and says: "No 'I,' no 'have,' no 'being,'" and so on, "there's no way to go on." Beckett's own words seem to parallel the final despair of the unnamable: "perhaps they have carried me to the threshold of my story, before the door that opens on my story, that would surprise me, if it opens, it will be I, it will be the silence, where I am, I don't know, I'll never know, in the silence you don't know, you must go on, I can't go on, I'll go on."[7]

Who are "they" who have carried the unnamable to the threshold of his story? The various narrators who have preceded? Molloy and Malone, Mahood, Worm, as well as the earlier incarnations of Murphy, and Watt? Speaking of Mahood, his temporary cipher, the unnamable remarks: "Before him there were others, taking themselves for me, it must be a sinecure handed down from generation to generation" (U, 315). He refers to Mahood as well as the others as "vice-existers" (ibid.), essentially occluding access to what must be said, to what or who is actually speaking. But these occlusions, the occlusions of names and masks, are but respites from an even more fundamental occlusion. In a phrase a few lines before the reference to Mahood and the others that at once evokes the scenic beginning of *Waiting for Godot* as well as a parody of Hegel's famous words about the spirit enduring death, winning its truth, the unnamable remarks: "allow me to think of myself as somewhere on a road, moving between a beginning and an end, gaining ground, losing ground, getting lost, but somehow in the long run making headway. *All lies*. I have nothing to do, that is to say nothing in particular. I have to speak, whatever that means. Having nothing to say, no words but the words of others, I have to speak. No one compels me to, there is no one, it's an accident, a fact" (U, 314, emphasis mine). He has nothing here but the "words of others," and the scene or setting of a road, the circumstance of gaining and losing ground, but getting somewhere—"all lies." An accident is indistinguishable from a fact; aptly evoking the circumstance of the Cartesian ego who can simply assert doubt as an absolute rule, the unnamable declares "nothing can lessen what remains to say, I have the ocean to drink, so there's an ocean then" (ibid.). Each effort, each word generated in order to end produces a new obstacle to be overcome: "I have an ocean to drink, so there's an ocean then." In the movement toward the end, toward completion—"with every inane word a little nearer to the last"—the end withdrawals, and the movement toward the end becomes instead the infinite detour of the end.

"You must go on, *I can't go on, I'll go on*." In the interview Beckett goes on to note that in the texts that followed, entitled collectively *Textes pour rien*, there "was an attempt to get out of the attitude of disintegration" but, as he remarks rather tersely, "it failed" (ibid.). In what direction was the attempt to get out of the attitude of disintegration aimed? Was it that Beckett sought initially to avoid disintegration, and wrote on in the hopes of ascending from this circumstance, only to fail over and over? Or was disintegration in some sense always the end or goal, repeated and ever more intense failures the point? Or was there something even more fundamental or essential beyond disintegration that was sought? To look more closely at Beckett's description of the end of his work reveals that the dust is indeed an end—"nothing but dust"—but an end no sooner arrived at than it too is deserted, given up—the namable. But desertion here is neither an abandonment nor a leaving behind, nor finally a passage to a more fundamental realm. Rather, desertion is a matter of something even more essential having to do with the disjunction between words and the absence of the world that the experience of words brings to light. Not just the absence of the world, or a world, but also the absence of language, the fact that in some sense what is being undertaken is a departure from the consolation of a "true" language that is still somehow connected to the world. The "namable" (dust) gives itself over to the immutability of the "unnamable" trace for which there is ultimately no word—"no 'I', no 'have', no 'being'"—in relation to which words and language remarkably perdures nonetheless. And in this we discover the ultimate paradox suffusing Beckett's work; on the one hand, resistant to language, to self-expression and dialectical incorporation, resistance can only be determined in the very language from which escape is sought. But the path of escape is continually obscured by the images, the voices, the figures, the characters and identities, the endless proliferation of shapes, narratives, and narrations, that suggest the outline of a legible and identifiable presence. "It's myself I hear," says the unnamable, "howling behind my dissertation. So not any old thing. Even Mahood's stories are not any old thing, though no less foreign, to what, to that unfamiliar native land of mine, as unfamiliar as that other where men come and go, and feel at home, on tracks they have made themselves" (U, 314). What is there, as Beckett reveals, is something excessive and illegible, not *a* world, unfamiliar behind or apart, but still very much a part of the void that in the Proust-like match-strike of illumination is at once revealed and withdrawn. What remains is a linguistic landscape made barren by the unrelenting process of violation that it has suffered, which remarkably enacts its own violation by remaining nonetheless, by holding to itself. Defenseless, denuded of significance and signification, what remains is interminable, inexhaustible, inevitable.

* * *

What Beckett is asking is "do we in fact know the language we speak"? We hear this in the terse opening of *The Unnamable*: "Where now? Who now? When now? Unquestioning. I, say I." The insistence of the questions of "where," "who," and "when," the traditional questions that govern the expectations of narrative and plot are raised, but no sooner raised than they are erased, made irrelevant by the word "unquestioning." But it is not just literary language, the language of plot and narrative that is put into question here; in addition, space (where?), being (who?), and time (when?), in short the philosophical prerequisites to a world, the grounds against which a self would ask of itself "who am I" or "what am I" are eliminated as well. But, as Beckett's opening makes clear, jettisoned or not, something remains, something or someone is doing the jettisoning: "Unquestioning. I, say I." This is Cartesian hyperbolic doubt turned back upon itself, and carried forth to its logical extreme. Let us consider the words again: "Where now? Who now? When now? Unquestioning. I, say I. Unbelieving." Are these two words, "unquestioning" and "unbelieving," that surround the determinations of the ego meant as adjectives describing the state of the self, of the "I" who says "I." Or are they meant as transitive verbs enacting a dismantling of the structures of belief and the logical predicates of the principle of sufficient reason? Or, lastly, are they simply meant as intransitive verbs characterizing a pure state of being and self? The answer is most likely all of these. The willed act of "unbelieving" generates the initial doubt against "where," "who," and "when," and leads further to the active "unquestioning" and "unbelieving." Still, something remains; the "I" of "I, say I." But as a verb this same unquestioning makes of the "I, say I," a fraud or conceit uttered idly in the face of nothing else left to say. Nevertheless, "unbelieving," it—who?—continues to speak: "Questions, hypotheses, call them that. Keep going, going on, call that going, call that on," all in a vain search for "me," for "I," or "who" or "what"?

The illusion of the unnamable's beginning from which the movement toward an end is begun is perfected in one of Beckett's late texts, *Worstward Ho*. The artifice is demonstrated as a singular and perhaps inevitable motivation to begin in order to end: "On. Say on. Be said on. Somehow on. Till nohow on."[8] Here, the voice (by this point in his career Beckett had long since abandoned the image of character), noting that it stands in proximity to an unreachable void, remarks enigmatically, "It stands. See in the dim void how at last it stands. . . . A place. Where none" (NO, 92). But seeing cannot see, and saying cannot say what stands in the dimness of the void, the place where none. What hope there is to become this place, this place "where none," this desert which is the place of place, the absolute itself is, after twenty-seven pages of the most unsparing prose, dashed: "Such last state. Latest state. Till somehow less in vain. Worse in vain. All gnawing to be naught. Never to be naught" (NO, 115).

The only language here is one of hypothesis, an imagined language, or the image of a language. The images of beginning—"On. Say on. Be said on.

Somehow on. Till nohow on."—and ending—"Such last state"—are given
in their expected places, their grounding registers intact. But the last state, as
the text indicates, is in fact not the last—"all gnawing to be naught"—not the
end, but only "such" last state, as if to suggest not the last but only the latest
state, barely discernible in fact from the state of the beginning which, at its
time or position, was itself quite possibly the "latest state."

Still, we are inclined to make things easier on ourselves, and presume
here a movement, a "progression," albeit a negative progression toward a
certain purity of expression and sight. But the situation is quite different
than this. "Never to be naught" because the situation, as he will write in the
dramatic work *A Piece of Monologue*, may simply be that "Birth was the death
of him. Again. Words are few. Dying too," and then, several lines later, "Dying
on. No more no less. No less. Less to die. Ever less."[9] Indeed, the paralysis
implied by the speaker's indecision—"no more no less"—is palpable until he
declares definitively "no less," as if to say that dying is always less, "ever less,"
though never final. To be born in this sense without an end that can be said or
conceived is already to be dead, and writing, which may begin as an attempt
to fill in this space that is void and lacking, only draws out the definitiveness
of this incomplete void and voiding space. Such, as the title of one of Beckett's
most uncompromising prose works suggests, may indeed be *how it is*.

* * *

Beckett's art is an art that aspires to be ever less, in the extreme to be
nothing—"only just almost never"—an art of zero. Virtually all of his works
unfold by way of bewildering processes of formation and deformation, serial
self-cancellation, affirmations deprived of content—"all I say cancels out"—
assertion and contradiction, willed impoverishment, all in a quest for perfect
stasis, impotence, nothing. In Raymond Federman's words, from one book
to the next Beckett's writing reveals "a deliberate process of disintegration"
that "reduces form and content, setting and characters, to a system whereby
composition takes place during decomposition."[10] This is indeed correct,
but the deliberateness of this movement or progress is paradoxically a
deliberate movement toward incompletion, apart from what could be called
in any traditional or *meaningful* sense progress or development. In Blanchot's
phrase, Beckett's writing is an "experiment without results, yet continuing
with increasing purity from book to book."[11] This purity for which Beckett's
writing continually strives, though, while it may indeed increase can never be
completed or realized fully; what could it mean to purely arrive at no result or
end? Things can be vanquished only so far. This is well known, though just as
well known is this: this is impossible. A hundred or so pages bound together
and set beneath the heading of a title, filled with words and sentences, spare
or not, can never be nothing. It must all, in the end, be something.

Beckett, though, was always aware of this. The assault against words, and the repudiation of grammar and style, as it is described in the 1937 letter, takes the following form: "Let us therefore act like that mad (?) mathematician who used a different principle of measurement at each step of his calculation" (D, 173). This is indeed an *undeveloping*, one designed to never end or arrive, as the principles of measurement can be altered, changed, reconceived and figured differently *ad infinitum*. Later, in the "Texts for Nothing," Beckett will suggest a similar paradox: "all you have to do is say you said nothing and so say nothing again."[12] The point to both of these statements, remarkable, even astonishing as it may seem, is that even when saying nothing it must all in the end be something, if only because it was said in the first place, and the only recourse is to say nothing, and then say it again, and again, because nothing, inanity can always be transformed into something. In *Waiting for Godot* Didi remarks "this is all becoming really insignificant," to which Gogo responds, "Not enough."

If there is any sort of systematic undoing or undeveloping in Beckett's writing, it is one that proceeds through the dilemmas proposed in the Cartesian splitting of the subject and object where the subjective will assumes a preeminance, exceeding even the fundamental grounds of self-knowledge, the *cogito*, such that doubt is indeed absolute. Am I speaking? It appears that I am, but *am I*? On what ground or basis may I declare that *I am* speaking. At best, it appears that *I am* a hunch, a bet, and not altogether a good one. This is the register of the unnamable, that for which there is no name, no pronoun, no verb, no case. In short the howling silence of a self and mind cut adrift, permitted to assume its absolute prerogatives of willful annihilation up to and including the point of itself. And still something remains.

In the "Texts for Nothing," we read: "How many hours to go, before the next silence, they are not hours, it will not be silence, how many hours still, before the next silence? Ah to know for sure, to know that this thing has no end, this thing, this thing, this farrago of silence and words, of silence that is not silence and barely murmured words. Or to know it's life still, a form of life, ordained to end, as others ended and will end, till life ends, in all its forms. Words, mine was never more than that, than this pell-mell babel of silence and words, my viewless form described as ended, or to come, or still in progress, depending on the words" (CSP, 125). Who is this one who says "mine," who says my life was never more than "words," who says the hours were not hours, the silences were not silence, but only their facsimiles? How even could one answer this question? Only with yet another word— him, or her, or I, or me, or someone, or *something*. Perhaps it's just life—life speaking, as if it, or this could—but then what is this if not also just a word? Here is the unsurpassable "attitude" of disintegration; but this realization— if it can even be termed this—still doesn't make for any sort of progression.

There are always more, or new, or different words, or forms and formations of words, forms of life. The attitude of disintegration is indeed inescapable, but that's of little consequence. In *Waiting for Godot* Estragon quips, "We are incapable of keeping silent," to which Vladimir immediately responds: "You're right, we're inexhaustible."[13] And with one certain affirmation, an entire world and existence can be deduced. After asserting his inability to control his bowels—I can't help it, gas escapes from my fundament on the least pretext" (M, 30)—Molloy takes up a count of exactly how many times per day he farts. The number at first appears excessive—"Three hundred and fifteen farts in nineteen hours" (ibid.)—but after some division it comes down to a mere "four farts every fifteen minutes," which he concludes is less than one every four minutes. "Extraordinary how mathematics help you to know yourself" (ibid.).

What Beckett is alluding to here and throughout is the strange temptation toward order and stability that always underlies the disintegrative attitude. Another system, another regime based upon different premises and axioms, is always possible—indeed all-too-possible. In *How It Is*, for example, we see a more ominous recognition of the inevitable recourse to forms of regularity and conformity in an otherwise chaotic and disintegrating world:

> at the instant I reach Pim another reaches Bem we are regulated
> thus our justice wills it thus fifty thousand couples again at the same
> instant the same everywhere with the same space between them it's
> mathematical it's our justice in this muck where all is identical our
> ways and way of fairing right leg right arm push pull.[14]

And throughout this austere, often decrepit tale of a voice with a body crawling, panting, murmuring across an endless mudflat toward his other, Pim, there are references to "dear figures," ratios of order, calculation, measurement; impositions that refer as much to the otherworldly scene itself as to the tripartite division of the text: "dear figures when all fails a few figures to wind up with part one before Pim the golden age the good moments" and then "sudden swerve therefore left it's preferable forty-five degrees and two yards straight line such is the force of habit then right angle and straight ahead four yards dear figures then left right angle and beeline four yards then right—right angle so on till Pim" (H, 47). It's dizzying. You follow it!

Such attentions to order and measure, though, are constantly repeated, here in *How It Is*, and in the other *residua*, "All Strange Away," "Imagination Dead Imagine," "Ping," *The Lost Ones*. Indeed, in these as well as the other later writings, the settings become increasingly strange and barren. We have departed the solipsistic confines of a self-contradicting "I," and its various locales—bed chambers, urns, jars, and so on—for ever more denuded and barren spaces: skulls, cylindrical enclosures mathematical in design, bare rooms, endless mudflats, unlocatable darkness in which silence becomes perfect company. What Beckett's minimal, and ultimately nonrepresentational settings in these later texts effect is a sharply drawn distinction between, on the one hand, a kind of minimal, but unrelenting presence, and on the other hand, an absence intimated, but never realized as such, between the regimes of order that make up the textual spaces and the world, the something up there. This is what is developed, intensified, extended to its most extreme. But it is ultimately the brute fact of the settings themselves, language-spaces as such, apart from any reference places or a world beyond or outside, that reveals the language as a space of absence. A place, to be certain, but a place that is no place inasmuch as it relentlessly signifies nothing other than itself and its own inexhaustibility, admitting of ever-more strange, but precise regimes of order. The increasing focus or turn inward in these writings, a turn that would seem to be the only viable alternative toward something sure and certain over against the realization that the external world and settings of conventional fiction are merely artifice, is in fact no less illusory than the external world of places and things. These inner worlds or domains—even when their dimensions are explicitly reported as in *The Lost Ones*, "inside a flattened cylinder fifty metres round and sixteen high for harmony"—are never truly accessible, they can never be reached or fully adumbrated. The measurements, precise though they may be, are only, as Beckett's text says, "for harmony."

But the same "harmony" extends to the figure or figures of the speaking self, I, or "I." Who, to paraphrase the question Maurice Blanchot asked in the late 1940s in reference to *The Unnamable*, is this I who says at the outset of *How It Is* "how it was I quote before Pim with Pim after Pim how it is three parts I say it as I hear it" (H, 7)? We don't know. We can't know. We'll never know. Apart from a reference to "voice once without quaqua on all sides then in me" (H, 7), there is no intimation anywhere of an identity that is separate from the movement of quotation that underwrites the entire text—"how it was I quote." But the source of the quotation, the original or originating voice now being quoted—"I say it as I hear it"—is absent as well, and if it is a narrative of recollection or memory, it is one without a genuine or reliable source, be it elsewhere or in the narrating voice: "what about it my memory we're talking of my memory not much that it's getting better that it's getting worse that things are coming back to me nothing is coming back to me but to conclude from that" (H, 15). At best all we can discern here is that the source is not I. But then who, or what?

This is an impossible text, without beginning or end save that which is arbitrarily invented. It begins: "How it was I quote before . . ." and so forth; and ends by declaring first that the entirety was false, the entire ordeal of crawling toward Pim, being with Pim, and then leaving Pim to await Bim, the figure for whom the narrator will now perform the same role Pim performed for it was false, it never happened, and then even more remarkably that the entirety could have been read or told in reverse. But within this strange narrative the relationship between the narrator and Pim, the sole object of the narration, is one of tormentor and victim. Finally reached, Pim, in part two, becomes the inert, speechless victim taught to speak by the narrator in a gruesome parody of pedagogy and communicative rationality. What *How It Is* displays is the possibility that orders and regimes are in no need whatsoever of a ground or foundation. A novel can, as it were, simply create itself, however strangely or paradoxically. More chilling, though, the invention of *How It Is* appears to run parallel to the same invention of orders and sequences, schemes of organization and hierarchy that define political reality. An order is always possible, because narrative inventiveness is strangely inexhaustible.

* * *

There's no getting past it except by an ever-more attentive vigilance. From a critical standpoint, we do well to take seriously what Beckett said in his essay on Joyce's Work in Progress, "Dante ... Bruno ... Vico ... Joyce," namely, that the "danger is in the neatness of identifications" where the reader-critic, involved endlessly in the process of tracing allusions and lines of influence in order to maintain the domesticated sight-lines of reading and understanding, becomes in effect, as William Carlos Williams suggested, a conservator of the past. Beckett says simply: "literary criticism is not book-keeping" (D, 19). The same point is made over and over in the writing; faced with this Nowhere and Nothing, the plight of the reader is addressed explicitly in the set of interpretive instructions offered by the unnamable in the form of the following introductory self-commentary: "What am I to do, what shall I do, what should I do in my situation, how proceed? By aporia pure and simple? Or by affirmations and negations invalidated as uttered, or sooner or later? Generally speaking. There must be other shifts. Otherwise it would be quite hopeless. But it is quite hopeless. I should mention before going any further, any further on, that I say aporia without knowing what it means" (U, 291). But with this said, proceed he does. As does Beckett.

Over the years since Beckett's writing first gained notoriety, a convention of sorts has grown around this predicament that states that Beckett's writing is steeped in a numbing "meaninglessness," leads nowhere, and is politically and ethically irresponsible and thus demands a critique and redressing according to the strictures of Lukács's social realism. Another version of this, slightly less polemical, is that his writing reflects a reductive and halting "absurdity" demanding interpretive silence. In both cases, however, these conclusions have been assumed too quickly. To say nothing or to remain silent in relation to Beckett's writing is in no way to come closer to interpretive or hermeneutic authenticity. And to claim "meaninglessness" as the "meaning," as Martin Esslin realized too late, defeats the very purpose of the claim.

The issue is that if in relation to Beckett's writings there is indeed an inability to say anything, then this inability paradoxically becomes the absolute imperative that we must say. For it has not yet been said. Or, having been said, it must be said again. It bears repeating. This is the lesson of *The Unnamable*. Meaninglessness cannot be asserted as the meaning of Beckett's texts, and silence before them is irresponsible. To speak bluntly, we don't yet deserve this. If this is indeed all meaningless, as so many seem to agree, then as Adorno remarked, it is "not because of the absence of meaning—then they [Beckett's texts] would be irrelevant—but because they debate meaning."[15] This, though, is precisely the point of frustration and confusion, for it would seem that in Beckett's writing the debate is endless, and moreover never undertaken in terms of one specific meaning over against another, never according to the specifics of one or another position. Rather, what is debated here is meaning as such, the *ideology of meaning* that proceeds from the basis of *ego cogito ergo sum*, but that in fact, as Beckett shows with an almost obsessive drive, is only the imaginary suturing that links cogito with sum. If meaninglessness is indeed the end—but it is in no way clear that this is so—then it is, as Adorno again puts it, an "evolved and thereby equally deserved meaninglessness" (AT, 221). And yet, the temptation to silence is immense. The last text of the *residua*, the last but certainly not the end, explicitly suggests this temptation by speaking only of the silence and the time still to come: "Such and much more such the hubbub in his mind so-called till nothing left from deep within but only ever fainter oh to end. No matter how no matter where, Time and grief and self so-called. Oh all to end" (CSP, 265). Such is the temptation of reading—"such and much more such"—and the time still to come, the time of the end, the time of completion is only a vague outline, a promissory note upon which payment may or may not follow. The book to be written on Beckett, despite the volumes already written and published, is still to come. It will always be this way. In the same way that the end, the last is constantly deferred and displaced by the very movement of words that would seek to arrive, to accomplish precisely this end, the book will also always be still to come.

These, in brief, are the reasons given by Beckett to speak, to say, and say again, to continue, if only in order to end, to get a little closer, to finish, to say what remains. What remains? Such is the difficulty of *writing on*, of writing toward, or to, or about the text of Beckett.

The lesson of Beckett, or so it would seem, is that meaning, even in the least conducive occasions and instances, is quite inescapable. And this is not simply an intellectual or an aesthetic issue. When we teach our children to write and develop arguments, to create and punctuate sentences correctly according to grammatical rules and regulae, or when our teachers produce finely developed rhetorical arguments, we affirm, by reproducing, a specific political state of affairs; political in the widest sense of the word in which the commonality of order and coherence are presumed, expectations of habit affirmed, and development proceeds as a natural outcome of the movement of thought as it appears and has appeared in the world. We speak of a "mother tongue," a cultural and cultured language, a language of thought, of reason; though when we repeat and reproduce this "mother tongue," we reproduce what Benjamin called the "habitual expression of its sterility."[16] This is what Beckett's writing is resisting. And yet, while it is possible to assert that the resistance to this ordered and ordering development is political, the actual political implications of this resistance are unclear, and moreover must remain necessarily so. The unnamable puts it thus: "The thing to avoid, I don't know why, is the spirit of system." It would be one thing to avoid or resist the spirit of system on the basis of a certain awareness, a conscious and intended resistance that would in effect be to replace one order with another, but it is an entirely different, and ultimately more challenging matter to avoid system for who knows what reason. And in this, in its resistance to development, a resistance that is actually an outright refusal of that process whereby the continuity of narrative, of developed and developing language according to certain regimes of organization is refused, we find a refusal not only of an intellectual and artistic order, but a political state of affairs as well. The "meanings" that assert themselves in political terms are not immune from this self-same grafting. Politics and the languages of politics are but one and the same; each bespeak a kind of organization, an adaptation in language according to certain rules to conditions and circumstances. The rules, though, are the issue. For they are endlessly adaptable. Molloy can organize himself according to the temporality of his gaseous discharges, or, as the famous stone sucking episode reveals, he can spend his time devising schemes by which to rotate sixteen stones in a circulating movement from his pockets to his mouth—"extraordinary how mathematics help you to know yourself."

A writing—be it fictional or critical—that would proceed according to a presumption of either originality or a seamless grounding within the fabric of a national literature becomes violent, even murderous with respect to the otherness of the world and the experience it seeks to portray. In this scheme or system of valuation each, to return for a moment to the Proust study, "counts for nothing" and are reduced simply to the level of a "notion" (P, 53). The decompositions of conventional reality rendered in Swann's flights of involuntary fantasy actually result in a voluntaristic reuniting, albeit in the imaginative faculty of the now detached and isolated artist. Hence, Beckett's paradoxical proclamation: "The artistic tendency is not expansive, but a contraction. Art is the apotheosis of solitude," where solitude serves to magnify and bring into sharp focus the impossibility of authentic expression (P, 64). "Even on the rare occasions," Beckett continues, "when word and gesture happen to be valid expressions of personality they lose their significance on their passage through the cataract of the personality that is opposed to them. Either we speak and act for ourselves—in which case speech and action are distorted . . . or else we speak and act for others in which we speak and act a lie. . . . We are alone. We cannot know and cannot be known" (P, 64).

* * *

This is one implication of Beckett's apothegmatized phrase "imagination dead imagine," to cite one of the later *residua*. The piece begins: "No trace anywhere of life, you say, pah, no difficulty there, imagination not dead yet, yes, dead, good, imagination dead imagine" (CSP, 182). In addition to much else, there is at once a warning and an urging in these words; a warning: beware, "no trace anywhere of life," no trace of the Word, no trace of that animating power out of which develops the belief in content and intrinsic meaning, the unifying transcendent mediation of language and the word; and an urging: go ahead, speak, write, indeed you must, you have no choice. The next sentence makes this explicit: "Islands, waters, azure, verdure, one glimpse and vanished, endlessly, omit" (CSP, 182). An image is forming. That animistic power whereby language annexes and makes over the world in its image is in play. But it vanishes: "one glimpse and vanished." The object or objects—"islands, waters"—and their respective colors are seen, duly noted, and taken over in the artistic vision that isolates and detaches things from their utility in the world in order to make them *useful* for art; then elevated by the fluidity of stylization—"azure, verdure"—through which the objects become image, become art. But this isolation of objects from their quotidian schemes, this solitude is not enough; true seeing, true perception begins only when the object seen has been lost, dissolved completely. Thus far, though, the notions of value and utility are still intact. One reads these words only at the point when the image, the image qua image, disappears behind yet another image, that of words, the neutral point where it all becomes nothing revealed. But not forever, not definitively or finally; rather "endlessly." The quest to see is endless. There's no victory. The last words of the passage "endlessly, omit," separated as they are by a comma, give us to see the glimpse and the vanishing both as "endless," and the process of cancellation as similarly "endless." And the two neatly divided impulses, the one toward a kind of linguistic fabulation, the other toward silence and nothingness—"endlessly, omit"— coexist simultaneously.

The impossibility of stopping is even more pronounced in the companion piece to "Imagination Dead Imagine" entitled "Ping." Here a voice utters a series of murmured phrases, vaguely asserting a congruence of shape, form, and sound: "All known all white bare white body fixed," and "Legs joined like sewn heels," "Eyes alone," "Head haught," "White ceiling never seen ping of old only just almost never," "ping of old perhaps there," "ping of old only just perhaps a meaning a nature." The disposition here of images—legs, eyes, a ceiling, a head, and so on—produces, or threatens to produce, however faintly, an image of a naked human being alone in a room. However, as the image comes closer to becoming fully realized, and thus closer to establishing itself as a meaningful entity, the occurrences of "ping" become more frequent, more insistent. Over against the illusion of fiction, the image of the Word, the sound/concept/word "ping" ceaselessly interrupts the flow and permutations of the utterances to act as a sort of nonsensical commentary upon the flow of the narrative. Sometimes, though, it appears sown into the movement as if it was "something," as if it was a discernible element belonging both to the time and space of the narrative—"ping of old perhaps there" and "ping of old only just perhaps a meaning a nature." But what is, or could be "ping of old"? The answer is arrestingly simple; the text says: "only just perhaps a meaning a nature." The image, as it is unfolded in the story, finally lapses at the precipice of materializing: "traces blurs signs no meaning" and "ping silence over ping" (CSP, 193). Ping is simply ping. No more, though most definitely no less.

"Ping" belongs, however strangely, to a level of language at which, or within which one speaks of fiction. What we may say is that it belongs to the metalanguage of commentary and criticism that continually breaks and ruptures the surface of fiction; here, though, this metalanguage, emptied of semantic and lexical content, has nevertheless become part of the movement of the fiction itself, taken over to reveal that the language of fiction, of art, was always animated by the secret incorporation of a metalanguage, itself a fiction. The repetitions and variations of phrases throughout the narrative, and the increased insistence of "ping" in relation to the figure or image of this naked human begins to replace the subject, "I," with the object/nonobject "ping." And, in the course of this movement, this progression of diminishment, the language of *ego cogito ergo sum* is being made over into that of *cogitat ergo est*, and the central drama or tension is concerned with the effort to join *ego* with *sum*. Although strictly speaking there is no drama—how could there be?—because there is in fact no character, certainly little or no development in the traditional sense, no place, or setting, no time even, and no plot per se. The ventriloquist has revealed the dummy as a dummy, and now remarkably refuses to speak.

* * *

In 1949 Beckett, along with George Duthuit, published a small, enigmatic text entitled *Three Dialogues*. In it, Beckett and his interlocutor discuss a number of different artists, the nature of art, its potency, and its possibilities. What Beckett had to say on the issue of the so-called revolutionaries of modern art is informative. Of them he says:

> Among those whom we call great artists I can think of none whose concern was not predominantly with his expressive possibilities, those of his vehicle, those of humanity . . . they never stirred from the field of the possible, however much they may have enlarged it. The only thing disturbed by the revolutionaries . . . is a certain order on the plane of the feasible. (D, 139, 142)

The concern here with "expressive possibilities" and "humanity" again asserts the view of culture as a force of accumulation, as vehemently "result oriented." Though it adds to this the basically humanist foundation of culture, the notion that humanity is what culture reflects and values, that progress is continuous, and can be drawn in the shape of an inexhaustible human face. What Beckett refers to here as the "domain of the feasible" is a domain where expression is equated with power, the *power-to*, the power to express, the power to express much, or little, or finely, or in the end truly. It is this potency to express toward which Beckett's attentions are directed. To his interlocutor's somewhat bemused question, "What other plane can there be for the maker?" Beckett concedes: "Logically none," but then continues, "yet I speak of an art . . . weary of its puny exploits, weary of pretending to be able, of being able, of doing a little better the same old thing, of going a little further along a dreary road." To the interlocutor's next question, "Preferring what?" Beckett responds, in the oft-quoted phrase: "the expression that there is nothing to express, nothing with which to express, nothing from which to express, no power to express, no desire to express, together with the obligation to express." The interlocutor's response, "but that is a violently extreme and personal point of view," is no doubt correct. Beckett says nothing to this, and the interlocutor concludes that "perhaps that is enough for today."[17]

The apparent contradiction of the imperative to express under the *inderdit* that there is nothing *to* express, is contradictory only if one accepts the conventional but stale premise that art is indeed always and only expressive, that its essence and being, as well as its value, lies in the degree to which it is expressive of a culture, that it be expressive of a subject, expressive of man. But at the same time, as Beckett's interlocutor asks, what else can there be, what other plane is possible? Beckett's answer is as succinct as it is limiting— "logically none." However, the issue here, as elsewhere in Beckett's writing, is not one of logic, nor of success or failure in relation to the precepts of logic, nor of a means to achieve a successful inexpressiveness by evading the habitual repetition of the "expressive possibilities" of art. Such an escape is not possible. Rather, as Beckett also declares in the *Three Dialogues*, what is at stake is the recognition that "to be an artist is to fail, as no other dare fail, that failure is his world and the shrink from it desertion, art and craft, good housekeeping, living" (D, 145). Failure is the essential domain of the artist. And for those who make concessions, firstly with the presumption that there is something rather than nothing to be said, and secondly, and necessarily, with the cultural institutions that endorse such expressions, their lot becomes merely "good housekeeping, living," doing a little better the same old thing. In *Molloy* this same point is made in slightly more ironic terms: "I have never been particularly resolute, I mean given to resolutions, but rather inclined to plunge headlong into the shit.... But from this leaning too I derived scant satisfaction and if I have never quite got rid of it, it is not for want of trying. The fact is, it seems, that the most you can hope is to be a little less, in the end, the creature you were in the beginning, and the middle" (M, 32).

Given the alternatives, either a complete escape—in which case one would have to remain silent—or an artistic housekeeping enterprise, or the seemingly resigned conclusion to simply hope to be a little less in the end, it would appear that there is little likelihood of any sort of real sundering or separation from contexts. But the issue here seems to be less one of political contestation than one of recognizing the epistemic condition within which political realities are fashioned. They, like identity in general, are impostures of language, inevitable fictions of a cultural imagination that desires to maintain the illusions of its life amidst the endless flow of an insurmountable death. Logically, however, there is no other alternative, no recourse except to concession, "good housekeeping, living."

In all of this there is an intentional contradiction. If what is preferred, as Beckett's epigrammatic remark suggests, is "the expression that there is nothing to express," this preference nonetheless falters at the very limit of expression. There is no possibility of such an expression. None is presumed. Logically, from the grounding perspective wherein the principles of identity and noncontradiction secure the ground from which we speak, no other perspective for the maker of art can be presumed or achieved. And Beckett readily admits this. The failure, then, given the tenet, becomes one of monumental proportion, for failure can never be complete; to fail completely, given that failure is the stated end, would paradoxically be to succeed, to accomplish, to say and thus contribute to the cumulative storehouse that is culture. Thus the oft-quoted phrase from Company: "No matter. Try again. Fail again. Fail better."[18]

This is not, as some would have it, a purely cynical, or "apolitical" program. On the contrary, engaged here is a subversive unsettling of the idealist basis of the language of philosophy and the social, historical, aesthetic, and political frame work this language both institutes and maintains. Within the cultural context, and in relation to the various debates today surrounding the question of cultural politics, and the politics of culture, Beckett's art must and does appear violent, for it is fundamentally an art of questions, relentless and excessive; it questions itself, challenges its own existence as well as the existence of what is defined as art in general. The word games of *Watt*, or Molloy's desultory wanderings, or the endless bickering of Hamm and Clov, and the various narratives of the *residua*, these are all struggles for survival, struggles to stay afloat, to not be swallowed whole. By what? By death? No. By tedium, by what Rimbaud referred to as the long march, the boredom of meaning, of progress, all of which is worse than death.

Politically, this is an interruption, a cut; more than simply a grotesque perversion in the tidy orderings of things, it becomes a radical intervention that makes order unrecognizable; or, alternatively, all-too-recognizable as an artifice of power and control. What Beckett's writing, in its vigilance and attentiveness proposes are breaks with normality and normalization that hold out the possibility for a different, though necessarily unimaginable kind of form.

What Beckett's writing enacts, though in reverse, is the catastrophe of inexhaustible significance where there is in fact none. And yet what he also reveals is that this catastrophe itself can never be spoken, can never be said, precisely because it is the catastrophe of speech, of the excess of violence that is speech that is silent. This catastrophe, whose name is to be spoken only in silence, as Adorno reminds us, is the ultimate, the last catastrophe, before which everything else is penultimate.[19] But it is last neither because of its temporal position, nor its magnitude, nor because it is the most horrific or unimaginable. It is last precisely because it is also and at the same time first, and thus is that point from which there is no step beyond. The horror consists in this: that its point can only be illuminated in thought, grasped retrospectively, after the fact, and in such a way that only reveals the paucity of thought in relation to the singularity of catastrophe. The point is too sharp, the wound potentially too deep, to be held within the omnivorous movement of thought without at the same time piercing the very limits within which this movement institutes itself. Beckett's writing, at once prophetic and comedic, evokes this limit with a precision virtually matching that of its occasion. We hear it in the first line of the play *Waiting for Godot*, "Nothing to be done." In Vladimir's profound hearing of Estragon's "Nothing to be done," we see the comedy of a human face that cries before the banal struggle to remove a boot. "Nothing to be done."

* * *

Beckett's writings are a progress toward night, toward nothing, toward where, as it was said in *Molloy*, "all grows dim." The progress, though, is slow going, interminable in fact. The radicality of these writings consists in their refusal of the search for a common order, for coherence, for meaningfulness, in their defiance of what is termed the natural movement of thought, and the calculus of utility that is the legacy of Hegelianism within which everything is put to use, within which everything has value and functions on behalf of the ideals of progress, development.

In this regard, consider what Beckett had to say concerning the relationship of his own work to that of Joyce:

> With Joyce the difference is that Joyce is a superb manipulator of material—perhaps the greatest. He was making words do the absolute maximum of work. There isn't a syllable that's superfluous. . . . He's rending toward omniscience and omnipotence as an artist. I'm working with impotence, ignorance. I don't think impotence has been exploited in the past. There seems to be a kind of aesthetic axiom that expression is achievement—must be an achievement. My little exploration is that whole zone of being that has always been set aside by artists as something unusable— as something by definition incompatible with art.[20]

For the time being, let us pass over the question of how impotence, which has not "been exploited in the past," could in fact be exploited at all (indeed, what might it mean to work with, or, *exploit* impotence?). Beckett's remark indicates that his work is concerned with what has been "set aside by artists as something unusable—as something *by definition* incompatible with art." The seemingly slight qualification, "*by definition*," is in fact anything but; for it alludes precisely to the point or points of intersection at which art joins with a certain notion, or *definition* of culture from which it derives its own sense of being and definition, and in a reciprocal imperative becomes one of the principle modes of a culture's own self-validation. What is valuable to a culture are achievements, the sum of measurable, calculable accomplishments that may be taken into the movement of progress in order to ensure a seamless flow of past into present, what Rimbaud scornfully referred to as "the march, the burden, the desert, boredom." Indeed, like Rimbaud—but we could also include here Baudelaire, Mallarmé—Beckett's writing is an attempt, as he himself says, to unleash that within literature and literary experience which alienates it from all forms of culture, and to suggest a line of access to what is outside the defining grasps of a culture or its adherents.

Indeed, virtually from the very beginning, and in everything that comes after, Beckett's writing has been and continues to be a challenge to the scope and range (in the end, we may have to say the ideology) of critical discourse, and the shock of this *oeuvre* consists, at least in part, in the ways in which it defies our long-ingrained habits of reading, habits of thinking, of speaking. It demands a critical language stripped of its proleptic commitments to meaning, and a termination of the long-standing allegiance to the negative progression of history and culture that Western thought has held sacred as the basis of its power and singular access to reality. "If I were in the unenviable position of having to study my work," Beckett remarked in a 1967 letter, "my points of departure would be 'Naught is more real . . .' and the '*Ubi nihil vale . . .*'" (D, 113).

Notes

I wish to thank Henry Sussman and Raymond Federman for commenting upon an earlier draft of this essay. I want also to thank Jennifer Caruso for being the respondent and the members of the Graduate Group in Theory at SUNY Buffalo before whom I presented a shortened version of this essay.

1. *Disjecta*, ed. Ruby Cohn (New York: Grove Press, 1984), p. 173, hereafter referred to in the text as D.

2. Richard Coe, *Samuel Beckett* (New York: Grove Press, 1969), p. 14.

3. Marjorie Perloff, *Poetic License: Essays on Modernist and Postmodern Lyric* (Evanston, Ill.: Northwestern University Press, 1990), pp. 161–62.

4. Gustave Flaubert, letter to Louis Bonenfant, December 12, 1856, in *Correspondance*, ed. Jean Bruneau (Paris: Gallimard, 1980), vol. 2, p. 652.

5. Samuel Beckett, *Proust and Three Dialogues* (London: John Calder, 1965), p. 20. Hereafter cited in the text as P.

6. "An Interview with Beckett," by Israel Shenker, in *Samuel Beckett: The Critical Heritage*, ed. Lawrence Graver and Raymond Federman (London: Routledge, Kegan Paul, 1979), p. 148. Hereafter cited in the text as CH.

7. Samuel Beckett, *Three Novels by Samuel Beckett: Molloy, Malone Diet, The Unnamable*, trans. Samuel Beckett (except for Molloy which was translated in collaboration with Patrick Bowles) (New York: Grove Press, 1958), p. 414. Though the novels were published separately, both in their original French versions and later in their English versions, the English edition has gathered all three of the novels in one volume to which I will refer throughout. However, for the sake of clarity I will refer to the individual novels separately, using the pagination from the collected volume, under the following abbreviations M for *Molloy*; MD for *Malone Dies*; and U for *The Unnamable*.

8. Samuel Beckett, *Worstward Ho* in *Nohow On: Company, Ill Seen Ill Said Worstward Ho*, ed. S. E. Gontarski (New York: Grove Press, 1996), p. 89. Hereafter referred to in the text as NO.

9. Samuel Beckett, "A Piece of Monologue," in *The Collected Shorter Plays of Samuel Beckett* (New York: Grove Weidenfeld, 1984), pp. 265–66.

10. Raymond Federman, *Journey to Chaos: Samuel Beckett's Early Fiction* (Berkeley: University of California Press, 1965), pp. 3–4.

11. Maurice Blanchot, "Where Now? Who Now?," in *On Contemporary Literature*, ed. Richard Kostelanetz (New York: Avon Books, 1964), p. 249.

12. Samuel Beckett, "Texts For Nothing, 6." in *Samuel Beckett. The Complete Short Prose*, ed. S. E. Gontarski (New York: Grove Press, 1995), p. 124. All references to Beckett's shorter prose will be taken from this volume and will be referred to in the text as CS.

13. Samuel Beckett, *Waiting for Godot* (New York: Grove Press, 1954), p. 40. Hereafter referred to in the text as WG.

14. Samuel Beckett, *How It Is* (New York: Grove Press, 1961), p. 112. Hereafter referred to in the text as H.

15. Theodor Adorno, *Aesthetic Theory* trans. C. Lenhardt (London: Routledge & Kegan Paul, 1984), pp. 220–21. Hereafter referred to in the text as AT.

16. Walter Benjamin, "One Way Street," in Walter Benjamin, *Reflections*, trans. Edmund Jephcott (New York: Schocken Books, 1986), p. 61.

17. Samuel Beckett, "Three Dialogues," in Samuel Beckett, *Disjecta: Miscellaneous Writings and a Dramatic Fragment*, ed. Ruby Cohn (London: John Calder, 1983), pp. 142, 139.

18. Samuel Beckett, *Company* in *Nohow On*, pp. 46, 89.

19. Theodor Adorno, *Notes to Literature*, vol. 1, trans. Sherry Weber Nicholsen (New York: Columbia University Press, 1991), p. 249.

20. Quoted in Raymond Federman, "Beckett and the Fiction of Mud," in *On Contemporary Literature*, ed. Richard Kostelanetz (New York: Avon Books, 1964), p. 257, emphasis mine.

LOIS GORDON

Waiting for Godot:
The Existential Dimension

VLADIMIR: All I know is that the hours are long, under these conditions, and constrain us to beguile them with proceedings which—how shall I say—which may at first sight seem reasonable, until they become a habit. You may say it is to prevent our reason from foundering. No doubt. But has it not long been straying in the night without end of the abyssal depths? That's what I sometimes wonder. You follow my reasoning?

ESTRAGON: . . . We are all born mad. Some remain so.

Waiting for Godot

Though human affairs are not worthy of great seriousness, it is yet necessary to be serious. . . . God alone is worthy of supreme seriousness, but man is God's plaything. . . . What then is the right way of living? Life must be lived as play, playing certain games, making sacrifices, singing and dancing, and then a man will be able to propitiate the gods, and defend himself against his enemies, and win in the contest.

Johan Huizinga

In a world devoid of belief systems, the mind and heart cry out for validation, for the assurance that life has meaning and actions have purpose. One may accept, as an existential truth, the assumption that despite the individual's

From *Reading* Godot, pp. 55–69, 182. © Yale University, 2002.

endeavors to comprehend or change the world, "there is no new thing under the sun" (Ecclesiastes), and, as Beckett puts it, "the tears of the world are a constant quantity...." But one also occupies a world of temporal measurement. Time passes and one ages, and, facing these inescapable facts, one journeys with tenacious will through the arbitrary divisions of time and space holding onto goals and belief systems as if they were absolute.

Life is not what the traditional dramatists portrayed, a series of ordered events with beginnings, middles, and ends. Neither are language and logic effective means for the communication and discernment of meaning. Nevertheless, the human creature, even if no longer motivated by the conviction of a divine mission, is continuously compelled toward purposeful activity. The need for a moral or spiritual anchor remains.

Waiting for Godot portrays both the need for purpose and the emotional fragmentation that accompanies the struggle for this anchoring of self. Vladimir and Estragon have inherited a world they cannot master, and despite their heroic accommodations they cannot escape the turmoil that accompanies their sense of purposelessness. It is as though an unfathomable anarchy had been loosed upon their inner world. Most of their efforts toward filling this emptiness reinforce their loss of energy and indecision and increase the disjuncture between their thoughts and actions. In reality, they are capable of participating only in temporarily meaningful action and fragmented communication. And they know this.

That they persist defines their courage; during their good moments they explain:

> ESTRAGON: I wasn't doing anything.
> VLADIMIR: Perhaps you weren't. But it's the way of doing it that counts, the way of doing it, if you want to go on living.
> ESTRAGON: I wasn't doing anything.
> VLADIMIR: You must be happy too, deep down....
> ESTRAGON: Would you say so? ...
> VLADIMIR: Say, I am happy.
> ESTRAGON: I am happy.
> VLADIMIR: So am I.
>
>   .   .   .
> ESTRAGON: So am I....
> VLADIMIR: Wait ... we embraced.... We were happy ... happy. What do we do now that we're happy ... Go on waiting ... waiting.

During their worst moments, boredom and ambivalence are replaced by anxiety and mutual intimidation: "There are times when I wonder if it wouldn't be better for us to part." Having searched the world for role models, for anything that might inspire a sense of purpose (and their conversations are filled with the wisdom of the ages), their quest remains unfulfilled. If their past has provided no codes or figures to respect or emulate, their future is similarly disheartening. They will inspire no disciples, peers, or children, for if they lack a coherent belief structure and sense of self, what legacy could they offer anyone else? Their repeated inability to act—"'Let's go.' (*They do not move.*)"—reflects their deepest awareness of their failed efforts to discern anything right or purposeful in life. In order to act, after all, one needs a sense of direction, of ideals or goals.

The paradox of survival in *Waiting for Godot* involves a rereading of Camus' "The Myth of Sisyphus." Sisyphus had the choice of abandoning his rock at the foot of the mountain or of continuously rolling it to the top, the only certainty being that after the rock fell, he could, if he so chose, once more perform this arduous, useless act. For Camus, Sisyphus's perseverance, in literal spite or contempt of the meaninglessness of his task, defined his superiority. By ignoring the irrationality of his fate and focusing on the blue of the sky and the texture of the rock, he could exult in his defiance of fate.

The paradox of Camus' Absurdism, like Sartre's Existentialism, demands a tension between engagement and impotence and between logic and absurdity, where the awareness of life's ultimate meaninglessness—*when placed at the recesses of the mind*—allows one to live fully and without anguish in a random and disordered universe. But Beckett's heroes differ from those of Camus: they lack a sense of defiance regarding their lot in life. One would never imagine a weary, disconsolate Sisyphus at the end of his rope, either literally or metaphorically; but this is Vladimir and Estragon's frequent situation.

Beckett's people also lack Sisyphus's most minimal assurances, for example, that the rock or the mountain will be present the next day or that time and space are as they appear. It is not only dubious as to whether Beckett's characters' most modest wishes can be fulfilled, but it is unclear if what they speak or hear is the intended message. They lack the most basic certainties upon which defiance depends, and this, along with their voluntary submersion of individual identity in role playing as a means of survival, makes them aliens in Sisyphus's world. The word *happiness*, used by Camus to finally describe Sisyphus, is, at best, only occasionally applicable to Beckett's figures.

Vladimir and Estragon's only certainty is the terrible uncertainty of the world, together with their accompanying need to assume that somehow and someday meaning will become manifest. That there must be a Godot who will provide this is the ultimate focus of their everyday activities, and in their pursuit of this hope lies the paradox of their busyness in waiting.

The very act of survival or waiting becomes Beckett's exposition of the games and rituals people construct in order to pass the hours and years, the accommodations they make to those closest in their lives, the alternation of hope and despair they endure in these accommodations, and the illusions and rejections of illusion that accompany each of these acts. Vladimir and Estragon's relationship is thus geared to distract them from boredom, to lift depression, and to fight paralysis. Although there are many other ways of surviving a world bereft of meaning, including work, family life, and social action, they have rejected these alternatives, despite scattered evidence in the play that they were onetime considerations. Vladimir and Estragon have also rejected the more self-indulgent roles that permit the outlet of anger and frustration, those less salutary emotions that accompany one's experience of the void. Masters like Pozzo and servants like Lucky pursue these less admirable roles, of the dictatorial sadist and submissive masochist; even for them, as Pozzo admits, "the road seems long when one journeys all alone." But Vladimir and Estragon assume a more humane relationship, one in which Vladimir assumes the more rational, philosophical role and Estragon the emotional, instinctual one; by so doing they can aspire to some egalitarian stability. They may pursue a relatively peaceful and predictable coexistence, unless, of course, something out of the ordinary disrupts their equanimity, something such as the intrusion of strangers like Lucky and Pozzo. Should this occur, as it does, their masks will fragment, and their less savory aspects will surface and rupture the equilibrium of their relationship.

The existential condition thus establishes the philosophical backdrop of the play, although Beckett neither answers nor systematically interrogates theoretical issues. It is in Beckett's rich depiction of both conscious and unconscious thought, the subject of future chapters, that *Godot* achieves its great intensity. That is, equally exposed in his characters' survival games is the emotional landscape in which their stratagems for survival function. This Beckett accomplishes by counterpointing the activities and efforts to manage each day with the feeling of emptiness and loneliness that motivates the well-patterned scenarios. Repeated objects, phrases, literary references, gestures, and spatial patterns—the mise-en-scène—become manifestations of the masked emotional life. In his emerging poetic images of hopelessness and despair, Beckett reveals the inner mind in counterpoint to the conscious efforts to survive. Dramatic conflict depends upon revelations about human nature within the context of the human condition.

First, Vladimir and Estragon appear as agents of free will; regardless of their doubts and despair about the future, they choose to live rather than the alternative. Unlike Camus' solitary Sisyphus, Beckett's journeymen have a companion for comfort or distraction; this may give them a better chance of surviving. But this is a complicated arrangement, for if their existential needs and emotional hunger necessitate their interdependence, defined by specific role play, these constructs betray them as well. Emotional needs continuously surface, and because role playing is, after all, an arbitrary accommodation to

the mess, the most carefully patterned script may produce identity confusion
and role reversals; at times, the scripts may fail completely. The plays's most
compelling moments occur when an authenticity of self emerges. Ultimately,
the insoluble problem is that each player has needs that will forever be unmet:
Vladimir will never have anyone to answer his philosophical inquiries, just
as Estragon will never have anyone to listen to his dreams. Thus, they await
Godot, unsure of who or what "he" is and entirely unsure of the outcome
of their awaited meeting. They are not disheartened over the possibility that
Godot may be a brute: they know, after all, that Godot beats the young
messenger boy, yet they still wait. It would be worthwhile if he came, even if
he abused them, so intense is their need for direction.

Godot, then, is that someone or something that would obviate the
need for the games that tentatively provide a purpose in life. Waiting is the
human condition, in which one constructs games or a lifestyle that mask the
unknowable. The name of Vladimir and Estragon's game is "To be or not to
be," and when they whisper or weep over this question, their words resound in
a void reminiscent of Ecclesiastes: "Vanity of vanities; all is vanity." That their
deepest dimensions of being prohibit any sense of peace recalls Hamlet's "I
could be bounded in a nutshell, and count myself a king of infinite space, were
it not that I have bad dreams." Confronted with such complex stage images,
we, the audience, engage *Waiting for Godot* with responses much like those of
Vladimir and Estragon. As we progress through the time of the play, we too
await a denouement, an intuition of meaning, Godot.

Staging the Existential

Waiting for Godot encompasses a sparse natural world—of animal (man),
mineral (the road and Estragon's mound or rock), and vegetable (Vladimir's
tree). Its two inhabitants perform the most basic functions: one or the
other eats, sleeps, urinates, exercises, dances, embraces the other, argues, or
sulks. They also think. Within the mysterious cycles of external nature (a
radish displacing a carrot) there seem to be intimations of a larger, equally
mysterious cosmic world (an unpredictable moon). In comprehending the
natural or supernatural, as the play's first line announces, there would seem to
be "Nothing to be done."

Lacking a social history or identity, *Godot*'s Everymen are being, or
existence without essence. They stand before us asking to be understood, as
they themselves try to understand, and they exist, as we respond to them, in a
context of virtual absence and its correlative, endless potentiality. Standing on
a road that similarly lacks definition in that it goes toward and has descended
from nowhere, they define themselves primarily in their relationship to one
other and with roles so well scripted that each is the other's audience: each

gives validation to the other's existence. Simultaneously, even while adhering to a script, each is the main actor in the scenario that plays out his life. That Vladimir and Estragon share the singularly most profound life goal, that is, of determining a purpose for living, is clear in the very name of their quest: Godot. If this refers to (a diminutive) God, the external world (cosmic or natural) might provide their much-needed rootedness. But Godot is also virtually a contraction of their nicknames, Gogo and Didi, the inner self that might alternatively give cohesion to their lives. As Gogo and Didi thus await an answer, an external or internal solution, it is natural, in moments of disorientation or disconnection, when they say, "Let's go" that they also return to their game with the ritualistic "We're waiting for Godot."

The universe in which they function reflects their identities and is a construct of how they envision it. The archetypal tree, rock, and lonely road lend themselves to multiple associations, some of which are ironic. The rock is not Sisyphean or Promethean; it is merely a place to sit; the tree, first skeletal and later blossoming, neither permits them a place to hang or crucify themselves in an effort to emulate the absent deity or simply to escape their failed lives; nor does it fulfill its function as the designated meeting place with Godot. The leaves of the tree, an ambiguous sign of regeneration or hope, become a symphony of voices that haunts them with elegies of past sojourners who similarly walked this lonely road. The most minimal objects in their possession recall other echoes of the historic and mythic past—all consumed with the question "To be or not to be?" To live is to think, and to think embraces all the voices of the silence. Peace or, more precisely, silence, as Beckett himself once stated, may be attained only in death.

Beckett mirrors the paradoxes of existentialism—the persistent need to act on precariously grounded stages—with the repeated absence of denouement in the enacted scenarios. Since much of act 1, with its series of miniplays, is repeated in the second act, which concludes with an implicit return to act 1, Beckett creates a never-ending series of incomplete plays within the larger drama, each of which lacks a resolving deus ex machina.

The paradox of purposive action and ultimate meaninglessness pervades. A deceptively simple boot routine is rationalized as purposeful activity:

> VLADIMIR: It'd pass the time.
> (*Estragon hesitates.*)
> I assure you, it'd be an occupation.
> ESTRAGON: A relaxation.
> VLADIMIR: A recreation.
> ESTRAGON: A relaxation.... We don't manage too badly, eh Didi, between the two of us? ... We always find something, eh Didi, to give us the impression we exist.

At times, their stoicism weakens. Routines fail to disguise the anguish of feeling (in Estragon) or of thinking (in Vladimir). Vladimir entreats Estragon to play his part: "Come on, Gogo, return the ball, can't you ... ?" Estragon must similarly encourage Vladimir: "That's the idea, let's make a little conversation." At some points, the couple finds it difficult to distract each other from "seeking," which implies the act of "finding" (there is "nothing to be found"), which would inevitably lead back to "thinking," which is, as they say, "the worst." Then, their exchanges, with multiple overtones from the Crucifixion to the Holocaust, follow:

> ESTRAGON: The best thing would be to kill me, like the other.
> VLADIMIR: What other? ...
> ESTRAGON: Like billions of others.
> VLADIMIR: (*sententious*) To every man his little cross.... Where are all these corpses from?
> ESTRAGON: These skeletons ...
> VLADIMIR: A charnel-house! A charnel-house!
> ESTRAGON: You don't have to look.
> VLADIMIR: You can't help looking.
> ESTRAGON: True.

Perhaps, they meditate, it might be best to just "hear" ("We are incapable of keeping silent"), although hearing brings back the voices of the leaves, their thoughts, and the past, whereupon they are thrust into the circular miasma of thought-frustration-rationalization. Their goal remains the ambitious: "to try to converse calmly" according to their well-performed script:

> ESTRAGON: So long as one knows.
> VLADIMIR: One can bide one's time.
> ESTRAGON: One knows what to expect.
> VLADIMIR: No further need to worry.
> ESTRAGON: Simply wait.
> VLADIMIR: We're used to it.

At times, they reveal the true subject of their game:

> VLADIMIR: Now what did we do yesterday? ...
> ESTRAGON: Yesterday evening we spent blathering about *nothing*. [emphasis added]

Even if these well-planned interchanges fail to adequately anesthetize them, there are workable alternatives. They can play with their words: "Calm

... cawm," "tray bong"; poke fun at, contradict, or create versions of their generic script: "That's the idea, let's contradict ourselves. . . . This is becoming really meaningless." Then their words can become like their hats, to be juggled to fill the void, another means of diffusing anxiety. As for their words as communicative tools, Vladimir and Estragon learned long ago that words not only are inadequate constructs for authentic experience but that, at best, they connect on different and variable wavelengths. The permutations and combinations regarding meaning are legion.

But Vladimir and Estragon remain exemplary in the elasticity of their absurd accommodation. Among their adversaries—the unknown, erratic, or uncontrollable forces—is logic, which appears to be more discrete and manageable than, say, such fateful events as physical debilitation or the sudden appearance of intruding strangers or any occurrence that might change their routine. Logic, after all, gives the impression of cohesion and viability. It seduces one toward feats of accomplishment; it helps in the pursuit of survival. It dictates coherence, indicating this, rather than that, course of action. It also gives one a sense of comfort, for it is a natural state of mind. And thus, Vladimir and Estragon's most ordinary routines, even their silliest vaudeville exchanges, like the bowler hat jostling, depend on the mechanics of logic, on continuity and causality. In fact, most of their interchanges depend on memory, which again depends on continuity and causality. If their games fail, they have emergency measures, which depend upon their past knowledge of one another and their anticipation of the other's response. Although a good deal of *Godot*'s humor arises from the two men's failure to enact simple tasks, like removing shoes and buttoning pants, and while habit may be a "great deadener" of anxiety, habit continues to demonstrate one's logic in a random and chaotic universe and provides the hope of linear and predictable behavior. As such, the characters insist on the truth or validity of their actions. Vladimir insists, "That's right," and when speaking of the limited human condition and need to help others, says, "It is true ... we are no less a credit to our species." Lucky also asserts that the content of his monologue is "established beyond all doubt," although Pozzo insists there is not a "word of truth" in a remark made to him. Vladimir similarly implores the messenger to tell them the truth, and because they receive the answer they expect, they grow more confused about their query than before they asked it. Even Vladimir, Beckett's logician, concludes his seemingly lucid "Was I sleeping?" speech by wondering: "But in all that what truth will there be?" Vladimir and Estragon's major logical problem is why their designated appointment with Godot never materializes.

Ultimately, Vladimir and Estragon doubt; therefore they exist, and in their most modest, mutually willed activities, just as in their responses to the gratuitous events that befall them, they are pawns of an undefined fate that determines the erratic efficacy of causality and any of logic's other manifestations.

Sensory experience is another adversary and dimension in the absurdist paradox. One would assume that, like logic, sense perception is natural and reliable. Yet when Estragon asks for a carrot and is given a turnip, Vladimir says, "Oh pardon! I could have sworn it was a carrot." Their most facile assumptions regarding the simplest of sense perceptions are uncertain: although Estragon is traditionally portrayed as the portlier of the two men, their conversation about the rope that might hang them suggests the reverse:

> ESTRAGON: Gogo light—bough not break—Gogo dead. Didi heavy—bough break—Didi alone. . . .
> VLADIMIR: But am I heavier than you?
> ESTRAGON: So you tell me. I don't know. There's an even chance. Or nearly.

The reality of human incapacity is nowhere more evident than in their use of language. The inability of words to communicate the most urgent of situations is underscored when each man cries for help and is treated much as though he had asked for the time of day. "Help me!" elicits the response, "It hurts?" So, too, even if language, logic, and the senses appear to hold, and the two try to assert their will, as Vladimir explains, one is not master of his moods. Thus, contradictions of word and mood are frequent, such as, "*Vladimir*: Don't touch me! Don't question me! Don't speak to me! Stay with me!" and "*Estragon*: I missed you . . . and at the same time I was happy."

Finally, there is time, the least comprehensible of their adversaries and perhaps the most terrifying. Despite their every effort, Vladimir and Estragon cannot deal with either mechanical or cosmic time. They can change neither themselves nor the world, which operates independently of them. To change would necessitate a sense of purpose, but because the world is indifferent in providing this, Vladimir and Estragon know well one of Beckett's axiomatic truths: In the absence of attainable goals or ideals, nothing, in a concrete way, can change. As Martin Esslin, who understood Beckett's sense of time, explains, "Waiting is to experience the action of time, which is constant change. And yet, as nothing real ever happens, that change in itself is an illusion. The ceaseless activity of time is self-defeating, purposeless, and therefore null and void. The more things change, the more they are the same. That is the terrible stability of the world."[1] Nevertheless, Beckett's play appears to move in a linear manner toward the future when Godot will arrive; and it is filled with traditional terms like *tomorrow* and *yesterday* and the colloquial exaggeration *a million years ago* and specifics like *in the nineties*. These, however, appropriately in an existential universe, function either in personal or in abstract terms. That is, in *Godot*, days, months, and even years pass in an instant; the tree blooms overnight; in what they believe is the next day, Pozzo and Lucky age; Pozzo is blind, Lucky, dumb. "When! When!" laments Pozzo. "Have you not done tormenting me with your accursed time?" Beckett's figures live out their lives before us existentially, and in their recurrent identification with historical and biblical figures they become archetypes of all humanity.

Time thus bends and contracts throughout *Godot*, as Beckett constructs a multidimensional tapestry of the human condition. One plays out one's life against a complex counterpoint of mechanical time (in which one ages and moves to death and obliteration), and cosmic time (in which one's acts have no function whatsoever). In the end, one's life is enacted within a universe that is indifferent yet autonomous—mysterious and stable, decaying and regenerative—a world of entropy and eternal renewal.

But time and space as existential or mechanical dimensions are further complicated by the psychological experience of them, and here Beckett stretches the paradoxes of human comprehensibility and adaptability even further. If, given the gratuitous events that require continuously adaptive stratagems, the will is continually self-renewing, the individual functions against an equally mysterious and autonomous force of the eternal unconscious, where time, space, and another sort of determinism operate in additionally mysterious configurations.

Thus portraying the multiple levels of psychological, existential, and mechanical time and space that are integral parts of his canvas, Beckett goes beyond the mere rejection of traditional narrative dramaturgy and character development to make space, time, the senses, and logic take on the dimensions of characters on stage. The forces that war with one another and determine the boundaries of human freedom are so complex and of such infinite power that he gives them a function once reserved for the Olympic deities in classical drama.

With the interplay of time and space so prominent in the play, it becomes very difficult to isolate the meaning and motivation of single words or lines because each demands an evaluation vis-à-vis all the others, and then a reevaluation within the multiple contexts of time and place in which each functions. The image of Chinese boxes within boxes is appropriate here, as Beckett's stage directions reinforce how, for example, a gesture performed in front of the tree or rock or an activity replayed multiple times may be both existentially unique and a variation of a single, constant emotional experience. Meaning *at that point* is dependent upon the spatial location in which it is enacted.

A single word may also reflect a different time and place in the speaker's life, depending upon which hat he is wearing or whether his pants are up or down. Meaning and motivation become as fluid and accretive as single words or gestures and function like isolated facets in a Cubist painting, in which the briefest sequence cuts across time and space, and the perceiver, with the power of associative or linear memory, juxtaposes the fragment against circular, vertical, or cosmic time. The part is thus integrated within the totality of the other facets and shifting planes of the design, like the circular or oval dimension of a teacup, which in its many-sidedness is impossible to represent on a flat canvas. Indeed, Beckett's manipulations of time and space recall a broad range of art, from the Impressionists to the Abstract and Geometrical Expressionists, in which vertical and horizontal time is simulated in order to convey the complexities of perception, logic, and final human incomprehensibility. *Godot*'s every word and gesture resounds in a void of silence, and the purity of Beckett's minimalist designs echoes with everything unsaid, the infinite polyphony and silence of the universe. The ultimate absurd paradox is that an indefinite possibility of meanings accrues to a world without definition.

NOTE

1. Martin Esslin, *The Theatre of the Absurd* (New York: Doubleday, 1961), 18–19.

GERRY DUKES

The Godot Phenomenon

Beckett wrote *En attendant Godot* in Paris, beginning on 9 October 1948 and concluding on 29 January 1949. The manuscript is contained in one notebook—a graph-paper school exercise copybook to be precise—which has not been generally available for inspection by scholars and academics. By all the accounts that have so far been produced the manuscript is clean and continuous with little evidence of hesitation or difficulty in the composition. This feature renders it very different from Beckett's novels or novellas in manuscript, many of which display, in the form of complex and complicated doodles and the like, that Beckett did not often experience the kind of ease of composition that characterises the manuscript of *En attendant Godot*. By Beckett's own account there were 'several' more stages to the compositional process before the first published edition of the play was issued by the Paris publisher, Les Éditions de Minuit, in October 1952.

The play opened at the Théâtre de Babylone in January 1953 and was greeted initially with some incomprehension and hostility. The players soldiered on and gradually the play acquired a cult status and became the 'must see' of the theatrical season. Barney Rosset of Grove Press in New York had already commissioned from Beckett a translation of the novel *Molloy* which Minuit had published in 1951 and, now that *En attendant Godot* was making a noise in the world, he began to press Beckett for a translation of the

From *Samuel Beckett 100 Years: Centenary Essays*, pp. 23–33. © RTÉ, 2006.

play. Beckett was unwilling to take it on because he was working intensively with the South African Paul Bowles on the translation of *Molloy* and he was also collaborating with Elmar Tophoven, a young German teacher who was working in Paris, on a translation of the play into German. The exact nature of this collaboration is not fully known yet but we may surmise that it arose from the fact that Tophoven's draft translation had used the Minuit 1952 edition as base text. While participating in the rehearsal process with the director Roger Blin (Blin also played Pozzo) Beckett had introduced numerous cuts, changes and the like to the text and he was committed to carrying the changes he made to the French text over to the German translation.

By late June 1953, however, Beckett had found the time to translate his play and he sent a copy to Barney Rosset at Grove Press and to various theatrical agencies in England and the United States. In an accompanying letter to Rosset he described the translation as 'rushed' and expressed his dissatisfaction with it. Nevertheless he undertook to revise his translation as soon as he could find the time. He travelled to Berlin in September for the premiere of *Wir Warten auf Godot* (as the play was then titled). In fact, by the time he got around to revising his 'rushed' version in November and December of 1953 between five and eight separate productions of his play were running in theatres across the Federal Republic of West Germany. The ironies cannot have been lost on Beckett, that one-time activist in the French Resistance—having struggled as a full-time writer, first in English and since 1945 in French, he became an overnight success in German.

The success of *Godot* in Germany should not surprise us. The Second World War, the dismemberment of Germany itself into East and West, the Nuremberg Trials, the Berlin Airlift, the beginning of the Cold War and the Marshall Aid programme were all recent events not yet forgotten, occluded or assuaged by post-war economic recovery. The figure of Pozzo, for example, with his unctuous assumption of superiority and exercise of arbitrary cruelty, would have resonated powerfully with a German audience. But *Godot* has resonated with audiences around the world and in many languages and continues to do so to this day. So we are dealing with a phenomenon that is not tied into particular or specific social or historical circumstances even though the play may well have its origins in Beckett's own experiences during the Second World War, as is evidenced by a small number of very specific details to be found in the original French version of the play. The references to the Ariège, to the river Durance, to the wine-maker Bonnelly just outside the village of Roussillon in the Vaucluse (where, as Vladimir says in the second act, 'Mais là-bas tout est rouge!'—'But down there everything is red!') all gesture towards landscapes and people that Beckett came to know as he hid from the Gestapo for over two years. Beckett, however, chose to cut or change. these specifics in the translation into English.

It was the late Vivian Mercier who memorably described *Godot* as a play in which 'nothing happens, twice'. This is far more than a smart critical remark; it is a profound insight into the very heart of Beckett's achievement in the play. For by the time he came to write *Waiting for Godot* Beckett's conception of what a play could be or should be had changed radically. A play is not designed to tell a story, point a moral or recruit its audience to a point of view, still less to a conviction or even an opinion. This had not always been the case. In the first two months of 1947 Beckett wrote (in French) his first full-length three-act play titled *Eleutheria* (the word means freedom in Greek). Copies of this play were circulating among theatrical producers in Paris at the same time as *Godot* was doing the same rounds. There were one or two expressions of interest in the play and Beckett even signed a contract for publication by Minuit. At the eleventh hour, so to speak, Beckett broke his contract with Minuit and refused to allow publication. That refusal stood right up to just before his death in 1989 when he insisted to Jérôme Lindon of Minuit that it was not to be published, even in the context of a projected *Complete Works*. Nevertheless, for reasons far too convoluted to go into here, the play has since been published in French and has been translated into English twice. *Eleutheria* is a curious work, more debate than drama. Its central character Victor Krap has retreated to a squalid bed-sit where he spends his time doing nothing and striving to be free and where he is intensively visited by many others—members of his family and their servants, his fiancée Olga Skunk, a glazier and his son. A spectator from the audience also gets in on the act, as does a Chinese torturer. In fact, *Eleutheria* anticipates by some years the kinds of situations and actions that came to be labelled as the Theatre of the Absurd. It is legitimate, if idle, to speculate what the impact would have been on Beckett's subsequent career as a writer if he had allowed publication of the play or had found a producer willing to take on the play that requires two sets—one of which has to be brushed aside into the orchestra pit for the third act—and seventeen members of cast. *Eleutheria* mixes French farce, vaudeville routines and slapstick comedy with some rather fraught and personal materials. It is my guess that he came to regard the mix as indigestible and simply withdrew the play. He gifted a copy of his typescript of the play to the American academic Lawrence Harvey in the sixties when Harvey was engaged on a critical study of Beckett's work as poet and critic. Later, in the eighties, he allowed a lengthy excerpt from the play to be published in a special number of the *Revue d'Esthétique* published to mark his eightieth birthday. At around this time he also undertook to translate the play for Barney Rosset, who had run into some business difficulties, but he gave up the task, as he said at the time, 'in disgust'.

What is literally astonishing about *Waiting for Godot* is that it is assembled out of very similar materials—comic turns, pratfalls, vaudeville—

but to much different effect and all deployed within a much tighter two-act structure. The principal difference between *Eleutheria* and *Waiting for Godot* is that the latter play has no point of view, it has nothing to say. This becomes very clear if we consider for a moment the play's pre-history. In late 1951 or early 1952, before publication in October of that year and ahead of the first performance in January 1953, Beckett's typescript was submitted to an office of the French Ministry of Education. There it was assessed and considered worthy of a small grant to assist it towards theatrical production. A radio producer with Radiodiffusion Française (a state-owned radio station) by the name of Michel Polac had access to all scripts that had attracted Ministry grants and he featured some of these in a bi-monthly radio programme. The programme usually consisted of selected scenes from the play performed after a brief introduction to the play by a critic or scholar and a statement about the work from its author. Beckett did in fact provide a statement but he deputed Roger Blin to read it on-air. The full text of Beckett's statement is carried on the back jacket of the current Minuit printing of *En attendant Godot*. It has also been translated into English twice, but not by Beckett. He claims that he put everything he knew about the characters and their situations into the play, that he knew next to nothing about the theatre, that the arrival of Pozzo and Lucky in both acts must have been arranged so as to break the monotony for the on-stage pair, Vladimir and Estragon.

In claiming to know next to nothing about the theatre Beckett was being economical with the truth. While he lived in rooms at Trinity College, first as a student in the twenties and then as a junior academic in the early thirties, he availed, on a regular basis, of opportunities to attend the Queen's and Abbey theatres and variety shows at the Royal and Olympia. His published criticism from the thirties and references in some of his letters all demonstrate a level of conversancy with theatre and plays in excess of the merely amateur. And, of course, he had helped to write and had performed in George Pelorson's spoof version of Corneille's *Le Cid* for Trinity's Modern Language Association at the Peacock Theatre, part of the Abbey Theatre, while he was a junior academic in Trinity in the early thirties. It is fair to say that he knew quite a bit about theatre before writing *Godot* and he put that knowledge to extraordinarily good use in writing the play.

The setting for the first act of *Godot* could hardly be less specific: *A country road. A tree. Evening.* The second act is set: *Next day. Same time. Same place.* The play is set nowhere in particular, which is tantamount to saying it can be set almost anywhere. This feature alone highlights the 'exportable' quality of the play; it is 'at home' wherever it is played. The scenic requirements are minimal—a suggestion of road, a bare tree in the first act (with the addition of a few bright green leaves for the second), a low mound (or a stone, according to the change that Beckett introduced for the production he directed at the Schiller Theater in Berlin in 1975). For the moon-rise that heralds the imminent end of both acts in that production Beckett specified a pale blue spotlight mounted on the end of a lever mechanism that inscribed a slow quarter circle as it rose behind the cyclorama that constituted the backcloth. The effect was eerie and cold and wonderfully theatrical because when the moon attained its full elevation it swayed gently for some moments, allowing the audience to intuit the nature of the mechanism that had hoisted the lamp. We should mention that the Gate Theatre production that will play in London and Dublin this centenary year is a very close relative of that 1975 Schiller production because the director, Walter Asmus, was Beckett's assistant in Berlin. Since that time Asmus has directed *Godot* numerous times and in quite a few languages and has found that the closer he keeps to Beckett's prescriptions the greater the expressive freedoms he and his casts can access. Beckett's own experience in the theatre impressed upon him the validity of the modernist aesthetic that less is always more, that the tighter the constraints the greater the urge to transcend them. In 1982 he turned this insight into a play called *Catastrophe* and dedicated it to a fellow playwright, Vaclav Havel, who was then undergoing the severe constraint of imprisonment.

Let's consider for a moment Beckett's approach to his characters, Vladimir and Estragon. He provides them with, at most, a very sketchy past. We are told that 'a million years ago, in the nineties' they were 'presentable' (the rushed 1953 version has 'respectable'), they both wear bowler hats—those relics of old decency also worn by Pozzo and Lucky—and when Vladimir tells Estragon he should have been a poet Estragon responds by saying: 'I was. [*Gesture towards his rags.*] Isn't that obvious.' So the pair have been together for a long time; they have come down in the world; they have worked as grape harvesters; they have no fixed abode—Estragon spent the night before 'in a ditch' where he was beaten 'as usual'. The play does not disclose where Vladimir spends his nights; all we can say is that the two men part company and meet again the following day, hence the semi-elaborate, almost ceremonial embraces exchanged at the beginning of both acts. While their past is sketchy their present admits of very low definition as well. As for their future, they have hopes of help and assistance from a man called Godot with whom or with one of his agents they have made an appointment to meet at the tree by the side of the road.

The appointment, however, like much else in the play, is contaminated by uncertainty. They are not sure that the tree they wait at is the right tree; they are unsure as to the precise date and time appointed but they are sure that if they fail to keep the appointment Godot or his agents will punish them. Nevertheless, towards the end of each act Godot or his agents dispatch a messenger to the waiting two to tell them that he cannot come today but surely tomorrow. The boy who delivers the message is the same in both acts though in the second act he denies this, suggesting that the earlier messenger may have been his brother. One of the clear inferences to be drawn from *Godot*'s deferral of the appointment is, as the cliché insists, that tomorrow never comes, it turns into today as a new one forms just over time's horizon, a threshold we can never cross. In one of his more piercing moments of lucidity in the first act Vladimir says of himself and Estragon that they have got rid of their rights. By making their endlessly deferred appointment they have effectively given themselves over to the power (if that is what it is) of the invisible Godot. All they can do in this circumstance is wait and while waiting endeavour to keep themselves entertained. This becomes increasingly difficult and fraught as their resources shrink and dwindle, waste and pine while the play takes its course so that the arrival of the other pair, Pozzo and Lucky, comes as a very welcome diversion. When they return in the second act the now blind Pozzo is led by Lucky on a much abbreviated rope. Lucky stops short at the sight of the other two, Pozzo blunders into him and knocks him down, Pozzo falls too and the pair sprawl on the stage, surrounded by the scattered baggage. Vladimir's response is interesting: 'Reinforcements at last!' he says. 'Now we're sure to see the evening out' Remembering the original title of the play, *En attendant Godot*, we now see that Vladimir and Estragon are, to use a French term, *attentistes*, literally those who wait.

The term had widespread currency in France during the war, especially among those who were active in the Resistance, not only in the German occupied territory but also in the Unoccupied Zone administered by the indigenous puppet fascist regime of Marshal Pétain. The term was hostile when it was not merely contemptuous and designated those who were content to put up with their circumstances, to grin and bear it, so to speak. Beckett was not one of those: he was active in Paris during the occupation and, after the security of the cell he worked for was breached and he fled south with his partner, he volunteered for the local *maquis* in the Vaucluse. Beckett was decorated by the provisional French government after the war but he insisted that his participation in the Resistance was 'boy scout stuff'. That may have been the case but many other non-nationals who had been active in the Resistance did not survive the war. Beckett chose to resist rather than to remain an *attentiste*, just as he chose to participate in the effort of the Irish Red Cross at the so-called Irish Hospital in the flattened town of Saint-Lo from August 1945 to the end of January in 1946. Unlike the vast majority of his fellow Irishmen, Beckett chose active resistance and participation in the post-war reconstruction rather than the insular neutrality that allowed them to be (as he put it some years later) 'simply limply republican'.

Beckett's distaste for authoritarianism, in all of its forms, is made manifest in the Pozzo/Lucky relationship. Initially this relationship seems straightforwardly brutal and cruel. Lucky, with a rope around his neck that tethers him to Pozzo, is burdened with baggage and is literally driven by Pozzo who is equipped with a whip. So Pozzo is a slave-driver and Lucky is his slave. During the lengthy passage of dialogue in the first act about why Lucky does not put down the bags even while he is at rest, Pozzo states that Lucky 'carries like a pig', 'it is not his job' and that he is bringing him to the fair where he hopes to get a good price for him. Vladimir's initial response is conventional: 'To treat a man . . . like that . . . I think that . . . no . . . a human being . . . no . ., it's a scandal!' And yet when Pozzo philosophises about the constant quantity of tears and laughter in the world he claims that he has gleaned these insights from Lucky, from whom he has learnt of 'Beauty, grace, truth of the first water.' A moment later he complains that the way Lucky goes on is intolerable and is 'killing' him. Vladimir, fickle as public opinion, rounds on Lucky: 'How dare you! It's abominable! Such a good master! Crucify him like that! After so many years! Really!' Six utterances punctuated by six exclamation marks, the final one the weakest of the set, suggest that Vladimir's initial response was merely knee-jerk and this one is as well. Vladimir's moral outrage directed towards Pozzo is easily redirected towards Lucky. If that is the case then his moral outrage is merely journalistic; it cannot be genuine.

It is the unfortunate, abused, burdened and exploited Lucky who, nevertheless, is permitted to deliver a speech which, though disjointed, fragmented, assembled from the remnants of various branches of wisdom and knowledge, articulates unpalatable truths about the human condition. Farcical authorities are cited, the 'Acacacacademy of Anthropopopometry'—that seat of wind and spatter—is invoked but the fact remains that man inevitably 'shrinks and dwindles', 'wastes and pines' despite the advances in 'alimentation and defecation', nutrition and waste management. We live in 'an abode of stones' that are more perdurable than we are—they were here before us and they will abide long after we have gone. While Lucky speaks the others become increasingly agitated and disquieted. All three throw themselves on Lucky and, when his hat is removed; he falls silent at last.

The return of Pozzo and Lucky in the second act is alarming, to say the least. Lucky is now dumb—he cannot even groan—and Pozzo is blind, or so he says. The pair seem to exist in a different order of time where to 'shrink and dwindle' are processes which have been accelerated, where degeneration and attrition are ineluctable. Lucky, who was driven by Pozzo, now leads him. The whirligig of time brings in his revenges. Pozzo, who in the first act consulted his watch so as finically to observe his schedule, now fulminates against 'accursed time'. His summarising image: 'They give birth astride the grave, the light gleams an instant, then it's night once more,' is as pithy, as depressing as anything in the Old Testament.

Beckett was disturbed by the fuss and confusion (his terms) generated by his play in the fifties and beyond. His view was simple, even programmatic.

A playwright composes a script; it is then realised in rehearsal with a director and cast and a technical crew. It is finally created in performance with a live audience. It is the audience that is the final creative ingredient or agent that completes the work. Beckett warmed to this notion in a letter to the American theatre director Alan Schneider in December 1957: 'My work is a matter of fundamental sounds (no joke intended), made as fully as possible, and I accept responsibility for nothing else. If people want to have headaches among the overtones, let them. And provide their own aspirin.' *Godot* has been particularly productive in inducing interpretative headaches. It has been seen as a post-holocaust play, a Christian allegory, a pessimistic fable, a nihilistic cry of despair, an indictment of an absconded God and, for the producer of its first American outing in Miami (of all places), 'the laugh sensation of two continents'. It is all of these things and none of them. It is what the members of the audience make of it, what they bring to it. *Waiting for Godot* is the mirror of your conscience.

RÓNÁN MCDONALD

Waiting for Godot

The scene, and the action (or lack of it), are unmistakable: a bare country road with a mound and a tree, two elderly tramps wait for their appointment with a man called Godot, who never comes. This spare, nondescript setting for Beckett's first performed play has become one of the iconic images not just of modern drama but of the twentieth century itself. The meaning of the play is less certain. One of the first questions that spectators of the play often ask is who (or what) is Godot? Perhaps he represents 'God'? The boy who appears at the end of each act claims that Godot has a long white beard, like some pictorial representations of God in the West (or like a child's image of God) and that he keeps sheep and goats. (According to the Gospel, God will separate the righteous from the damned by putting the 'sheep' on his right side, 'goats' on his left (Matthew 25: 32–3).) After all, Godot gives Estragon and Vladimir a sense of direction and purpose in their lives (however misplaced), in a manner analogous to religious belief. Could the play, then, be an allegory for a post-theistic existence? Written in the shadow of the Second World War, God/Godot seems to have deserted a world mutilated by barbarism, mass destruction and genocide. His absence has left a hole which unavailing desire and expectation vainly try to fill.

But caution is required here. Beckett's work always resists singular explanation. Beckett's answer to the question 'Who is Godot?' was always,

From *The Cambridge Introduction to Samuel Beckett*, pp. 29–43. © Rónán McDonald, 2006.

'If I knew, I would have said so in the play.' When the eminent actor Ralph Richardson, a prospective Vladimir in the first London production, inquired of Beckett if Godot was God, Beckett responded that had he meant God he would have said God and not Godot. Godot's name resembles, but at the same time is more than, 'God'. Given that the play is replete with biblical allusion and deals with fundamental issues of time, desire, habit, suffering and so on, it is not too extravagant to recognise a religious element to the play, and to the figure of Godot, while still drawing back from a complete identification.

There might be a lesson here as to how we might read the play as a whole. *Waiting for Godot* is full of suggestion, but it is not reducible to exact allegorical correspondence. Beckett described it as 'striving all the time to avoid definition'. The play will not be pinned down or located, a clear meaning will not arrive for us, just as Godot does not arrive for Vladimir and Estragon. They can be confused and uncertain about where they are, where they were and where they will be, and the audience, by extension, can feel bewildered by the elusive themes of a play which, while orbiting around philosophical and religious issues, tends to keep them at a distance, to keep us in a state of interpretative suspension.

To tie *Waiting for Godot* too closely to the religious metaphor might be to restrain its suggestive power. There are philosophical and psychological as well as theological dimensions to Godot's non-arrival. He can be seen to stand in for all striving, all hope, the tendency for us to live our lives geared towards some prospective attainment. Most human beings live in a constant state of yearning (low- or high-level) and fix onto some hope or desire for the future: the holiday just round the corner, the right job, the well-earned retirement. Once that hope is achieved or desire fulfilled, it moves on to some other object. As Beckett puts it in *Proust*,

> We are disappointed at the nullity of what we are pleased to call attainment. But what is attainment? The identification of the subject with the object of his desire? The subject has died—and perhaps many times—on the way. (P 13–14)

According to the pessimistic philosophy advanced in Beckett's early essay (heavily influenced, as it is, by the nineteenth-century German philosopher Arthur Schopenhauer), the self is fragmented and distended through time and is better understood as a series of selves. Once one ambition or urge is fulfilled, desire shifts promiscuously on to another prospective attainment. Ultimately it cannot be fulfilled: 'whatever the object, our thirst for possession is, by definition, insatiable' (17). Life then becomes about a vain, future-orientated expectation of a Godot who does not arrive. We fill our days with routines and habits in expectation of this arrival, rarely stopping to confront the desperate situation in which we live—the scarcity and provisionality of fulfilment, the terrible destructiveness of time, the inevitability of death from the very moment of birth ('the grave-digger puts on the forceps' (90–1)).

At least three features of the play, however, redeem this bleak and pessimistic view of life. First, there is a fellow-feeling and kindness between Estragon and Vladimir. Second, the play is extremely funny, with that distinctly Beckettian comedy—dark, daring, intelligent and disturbing—that has the same roots as tragedy, rather than simply providing comic relief from it. As Nell remarks in Beckett's next play, *Endgame*, 'nothing is funnier than unhappiness' (20). Third, the writing and theatrical structure are meticulously poised and often beautifully crafted. It is frequently the case in Beckett's work that the form, which is always so scrupulous, precise and painstaking, has a symmetry and a serenity which brushes against the seemingly chaotic and miserable life conditions that are being described. *Waiting for Godot* does not have the quasi-musical shapes and patterns of Beckett's later minimalist 'dramaticules'. But the dialogue and the action here have a precision and a spare beauty that, one could argue, counters the ostensibly pessimistic subject matter. Without these finely honed techniques, Beckett could not have taken drama into the unexplored territory of boredom and stasis, while still maintaining theatrical energy. This is a play after which world drama would never be the same again. Many commentators would now hold it up as the most important play of the twentieth century. Deservedly or not, it is the single work for which Beckett is most well known and the work that transformed him, at forty-seven years of age, from a relatively obscure experimental novelist into a figure of global cultural importance.

The question of what or who Godot might be is only one of the perplexities in a play replete with meanings withheld and explanations denied. It is a play which can still confound students and theatregoers, just as it did many of the initial audiences, who often responded with bewilderment and hostility. Why do the men seem incapable of leaving this spot? What separates the two acts? Why are there leaves on the tree in the second act but not the first? Why does Lucky allow himself to be so abused by Pozzo? What are we to make of the allusions to the crucifixion and to the Garden of Eden? It might be worth bearing in mind that the audience's lack of certainty is also shared by the two leads:

> ESTRAGON: We came here yesterday.
> VLADIMIR: Ah no, there you're mistaken.
> ESTRAGON: What did we do yesterday?
> VLADIMIR: What did we do yesterday?
> ESTRAGON: Yes.
> VLADIMIR: Why ... (*Angrily*) Nothing is certain when you're
>   about. (14)

The desperate unreliability of memory is reinforced in Act II, as Estragon and Vladimir once again falteringly try to figure out whether they were there the day before or not. Estragon, who is less certain and less interested in the past than Vladimir, can't recognise his boots in the middle of the stage. Vladimir is discomfited by the leaves that have appeared on the tree. It is partly as an antidote to this bewilderment that they embrace the one guiding principle of which they can be sure: 'What are we doing here, that is the question. And we are blessed in this, that we happen to know the answer. Yes, in this immense confusion one thing alone is clear. We are waiting for Godot to come—' (80).

From the audience's point of view, one effect of the lack of definition, the withholding of a clear meaning, is to shift the attention on to the dramatic qualities of the play rather than the significance of its message, its function rather than its meaning. It is clearly an innovatory and experimental play, removed from the conventions of naturalist drama. The notion of plot is fairly routed here. A clear relationship between cause and effect, the sequence of exposition, complication and resolution, is thwarted, as we would expect in a play which makes withheld knowledge not only its theme but also its method. That the second act is so suggestive of a repetition of the first (together with intimations that both 'days' might be part of an endless cycle) complicates the relationship of cause and effect, or the progression from beginning to middle to end, that audiences weaned on the well-made-play would expect. And the tightly knitted plot, where all the strands of the play are tied neatly into an intricate and satisfying pattern, is far more ragged here, with jokes and stories left unfinished, information continually withheld and events occurring with no seeming cause or connection. By whom and why does Estragon get beaten every night? When did the two men make their appointment to see Godot? Or is this just a figment of their unreliable memory? Why does Godot beat one of the boys but not his brother? Why was one of the thieves saved, but not the other? Why does Godot not come? We too will wait in vain for definitive answers to these questions.

In order to make theatre of this condition, Beckett must rewrite the rule-book, strive for a new grammar of the stage, more anti-dramatic than dramatic, which will resist exposition, climax and denouement and incarnate boredom, inaction and opacity. In order to understand his method, one could point at the very first line of the play, 'Nothing to be done' (9). Action presupposes a reasonably autonomous self and a world of intelligible causality, and, since neither is available in Beckett's plays, there is little action on his stage. Estragon's famous description of the play in which he appears—'Nothing happens, nobody comes, nobody goes, it's awful!' (41)—is wryly summed up by the critic Vivian Mercier's pithy quip that this is a play in which, 'nothing happens, twice', probably the most commonly quoted critical remark about *Waiting for Godot*.

But on the other hand is 'waiting' itself not a sort of action? To be sure the notion of action is here extended into an area previously deemed ineffective in the theatre. Inertia, punctuated with inconsequential dialogue, sustains a large part of the play. But, against Mercier, it is clearly not the case that *nothing* happens here. Even apart from the arrival of Pozzo and Lucky, which brings a welcome injection of energy into both acts, a range of movement and activity takes place: playing with boots, exchanging hats, trousers falling down, characters running on and off. Moreover, the conversation and physical exchanges between the two leads constitutes a sort of dramatic activity. Surely interaction cannot be so wholly severed from action? Yes, there is much that is trivial and uneventful—mocking the gestures towards religious and philosophical profundity—but there is action in this play. Not just action, but a lot of rather vivid farce occurs on stage, pratfalls and antics that we might associate with the music hall or vaudeville (one of the acknowledged popular influences on which the play draws).

Realist drama hides its fictive, theatrical nature in its efforts to reproduce the appearance of the 'real' world. But *Waiting for Godot* is theatre which continually declares its own theatrical artifice. The idea of play and of play-acting operates within it on a number of levels. First, we have many self-conscious performances, the idea that the dialogue between Vladimir and Estragon is a kind of a 'game': 'Come on, Gogo, return the ball, can't you, once in a way?' (12). The performative quality is especially evident in Act II, when, to pass the time as usual, the pair 'play' at being Pozzo and Lucky. This metatheatrical element—the play's awareness of itself as a play—refuses the suspension of disbelief central to realism on the stage. If Vladimir and Estragon can pretend to be Pozzo and Lucky, then how can we be sure that Pozzo and Lucky are not just doing the same thing? Given that this is a play, we know of course that they are doing so—actors are playing all five parts and will do so again and again until the end of the run. There are several suggestions that the two acts are part of an ongoing cycle, and not just because of the many similarities between both days on which the acts supposedly take place. At the end of Act I, Vladimir remarks that the appearance of Pozzo and Lucky has changed, as if he and Estragon have met them before. At the end of Act II, he anticipates that they will be returning to the same spot tomorrow. So, in a sense, the repetition in the play, the suggestion that the activities are part of an ongoing cycle, reproduces the repetition *of* the play, the fact that the play is put on night after night.

Most people's lives involve a cycle or a routine of some sort, whether this is as prosaic as the working day or the rituals of getting up, eating and going to bed. Most of us develop habits or recurring patterns of behaviour that we follow rather unreflectively until some crisis or unusual event in life breaks through them. 'Habit', Vladimir declares, 'is a great deadener' (91). So the idea of repetition resonates with a certain aspect of day-to-day life at its most remorselessly mundane. However, at the same time it obviously reflects what actually happens in a play: actors turning up night after night to deliver lines that they have delivered before and will deliver again. In this way *Waiting for Godot* brings its own status as a piece of theatre into thematic alignment with a pessimistic view of life as repetition and habit. If conventional realist drama strives to mirror life, then this play, by contrast, shows how much life mirrors drama.

There are other metatheatrical techniques in the play subtly integrated into the action and texture of the language. So we do not have characters marching on stage from the auditorium (as we do, say, in Beckett's *Eleutheria*, the Pirandellesque play he wrote just before *Waiting for Godot*, unpublished during his lifetime and as yet unperformed), but we do have lots of activity within the play which self-reflexively borrows theatrical language. So, for instance, Vladimir runs off-stage in answer to one of the urgent calls of his defective bladder and the two actors playfully pretend to be fellow spectators of a performance:

> ESTRAGON: End of the corridor, on the left
> VLADIMIR: Keep my seat.
> (*Exit Vladimir*) (35)

Throughout the play the characters make remarks, usually pejorative, about the way their exchanges are going: 'This is becoming really insignificant,' Vladimir disdainfully points out at one point (68). We also have more overt self-reflexive exchanges such as the following:

> VLADIMIR: Charming evening we're having.
> ESTRAGON: Unforgettable.
> VLADIMIR: And it's not over.
> ESTRAGON: Apparently not.
> VLADIMIR: It's only beginning.
> ESTRAGON: It's awful.
> VLADIMIR: Worse than the pantomime.
> ESTRAGON: The circus.
> VLADIMIR: The music-hall.
> ESTRAGON: The circus. (34–5)

This exchange is a comment on the sort of play-acting that the two vagrants get up to in order to pass the time while waiting for Godot. But at the same time as it passes judgement on these exchanges, it also forms a part of them—it is just such a music hall exchange itself. Furthermore it humorously operates as a parody of the sort of snobbish conversation that might take place in the bar of the theatre during the interval. This brings the performance on stage, with all its inherent pretence, into alignment with the pretence and affectations of the world off-stage. So, again, the stage here is not passively seeking to reproduce 'real life' in the manner of naturalist drama. Rather it is demonstrating how the pretences and repetitions of drama are themselves reflections of life. So *Waiting for Godot* is a play that does something more radical than simply bringing reality into a performance—it is showing the performative, theatrical and repetitive aspects of what we call reality.

Often these metatheatrical aspects to the play take on the quality of parody, especially when aimed at the jaded theatrical traditions that are being overturned. So, for instance, Pozzo's attempt at an elegy for the setting sun seems like a send-up of portentously lyrical or poetic language:

> It is pale and luminous like any sky at this hour of the day. (*Pause.*) In these latitudes. (*Pause.*) When the weather is fine. (*Lyrical.*) An hour ago (*he looks at his watch, prosaic*) roughly (*Lyrical*) having poured fourth ever since (*he hesitates, prosaic*) say ten o'clock in the morning (Lyrical) tirelessly torrents of red and white light it begins to lose its effulgence, to grow pale (*gestures of the two hands lapsing by stages*) pale, ever a little paler, a little paler until (*dramatic pause, ample gesture of the two hands flung wide apart*) pppfff! finished! it comes to rest. (37–8)

The intertwining of the pretentiously lyrical and the mundanely prosaic, here reinforced by the shifting stage directions, comically deflates this elegy. As Pozzo will bitterly come to realise when he himself is devastated by the ravages of time, loss and degeneration cannot be sweetened by pat lyrical eloquence.

There is a sense in which any language which strives to be over-expressive, whether in the lyricism of Pozzo or the philosophising of Lucky, is derided. Lucky's 'think' is a parody of academic rhetoric and the blunt instrument of theological and philosophical inquiry:

> Given the existence as uttered forth in the public works of Puncher and Wattmann of a personal God quaquaquaqua with white beard quaquaquaqua outside time without extension who from the heights of divine apathia divine athambia divine aphasia ... (42–3)

Showy soliloquy and bluntly abstract philosophical ideas are ungainly expressive mechanisms for Beckett. The key Beckettian principle, which will lead to the ever greater diminution and 'purification' of his work as he gets older, is that expressive language is not to be trusted, that shape and silence are where artistic impact lies. Even as early as 1937, long before his post-war revelation, Beckett has registered his dissatisfaction with language, his desire to find expressiveness in the spaces in between words. In a famous letter to Axel Kann, he speaks of his quest to tear holes in language: 'more and more my own language appears to me like a veil that must be torn apart in order to get at the things (or the Nothingness) behind it' (D 172). Not surprisingly, then, the most expressive moments in his plays often occur in the pauses and silences, indicating, at turns, repression, fear, anticipation or horrified inarticulacy. This pressing reality of the silence in *Waiting for Godot* is, as Beckett put it, 'pouring into this play like water into a sinking ship'. Much of what Beckett has to say in his drama lies in what is omitted, when his characters cannot muster the words or the play-acting to forestall the encroaching silence, or the 'dead voices' that haunt Vladimir and Estragon when they stop speaking:

ESTRAGON: In the meantime let us try and converse calmly,
    since we are incapable of keeping silent.
VLADIMIR: You're right, we're inexhaustible.
ESTRAGON: It's so we won't think.
VLADIMIR: We have that excuse.
ESTRAGON: It's so we won't hear.
VLADIMIR: We have our reasons.
ESTRAGON: All the dead voices.
VLADIMIR: They make a noise like wings.
ESTRAGON: Like leaves.
VLADIMIR: Like sand.
ESTRAGON: Like leaves.
    (*Silence.*)
VLADIMIR: They all speak together.
ESTRAGON: Each one to itself.
    (*Silence.*)
VLADIMIR: Rather they whisper.
ESTRAGON: They rustle.
VLADIMIR: They murmur.
ESTRAGON: They rustle.
    (*Silence.*)
[...]
VLADIMIR: They make a noise like feathers.
ESTRAGON: Like leaves.
VLADIMIR: Like ashes.
ESTRAGON: Like leaves.

(*Long silence.*)
VLADIMIR: Say something!
ESTRAGON: I'm trying.
(*Long silence.*)
VLADIMIR: (*In anguish.*) Say anything at all!
ESTRAGON: What do we do now?
VLADIMIR: Wait for Godot.
ESTRAGON: Ah!
(*Silence.*) (62–3)

The economic rhythms of this passage and the careful combinations of repetition and variation combine with a soothing susurration to eke out a compelling dissonance between the language and the characters' guilty torment. Vladimir and Estragon are too close: they listen to the dead voices while we listen to the poetry. Hence Vladimir's desperate 'Say something!' after the long silence at the end of the exchange. The passage does not express their torment directly, but rather catches those dead voices elliptically, in the excruciating pauses.

Here as elsewhere the exchanges have an eerie, pre-ordained quality, reinforcing the point about the performative, repetitive, self-consciously theatrical dimension to the play. It is as if when Vladimir says something Estragon's reply has already been decided (which of course it has, since both speak from a memorised play script). Their exchanges are often constituted of one- or two-word utterances, carefully shaped into repetition and variation, giving them a poetic, estranging quality that unsettles the colloquial banality. Nonetheless, performance in a theatre renders the *unsaid* as present as the said, and, for all their spare beauty, these carefully pruned exchanges are scarcely enough to block out an encroaching and terrifying silence. This is why, presumably, Estragon and Vladimir are so desperate to keep the conversation alive, to block out the sound of the dead voices. Or perhaps to keep back the realisation that the silence brings: their conversations, like the waiting games they play, are a futile distraction from the destructiveness of time and the insatiability of desire. They are merely a 'habit' which protects them from the stricken awareness of their own abjection and solitude:

VLADIMIR: All I know is that the hours are long, under these conditions, and constrain us to beguile them with proceedings which—how shall I say—which may at first sight seem reasonable, until they become a habit. (80)

'Habit', once again, is a 'great deadener'. It deadens the suffering that too much awareness, too much reflection on the conditions of existence would bring. The daily routines, the various distractions of conversation and play-acting, are forms of self-protection.

There are clear differences between the two tramps. Estragon is preoccupied with physicality, the body, the earth. Not insignificantly, he tends to sit down far more than Vladimir. He is obsessed with his boots, whereas Vladimir often inspects his hat. Vladimir thinks, Estragon feels. At rehearsal, Beckett remarked of the pair: 'Estragon is on the ground; he belongs to the stone. Vladimir is light; he is oriented towards the sky.' It is Vladimir who wonders about the two thieves crucified alongside 'Our Saviour', he who reflects on the nature of time at the end of the play. He who always answers Estragon's question about the purpose of their attendance at this spot:

> ESTRAGON: Let's go.
> VLADIMIR: We can't.
> ESTRAGON: Why not?
> VLADIMIR: We're waiting for Godot.
> ESTRAGON: Ah! (78)

It is Vladimir who addresses the young boy at the end of each act, who experiences the philosophical insights. Many spectators record the impression that the two tramps feel like an old married couple, who bicker and quarrel—'but for me . . . where would you be . . .?'; 'I'm tired telling you that'—and even threaten to leave each other. But underneath their irritations and impatience there is a close bond, and a recognition of their shared plight. 'We don't manage too badly, eh Didi, between the two of us?' (69). Vladimir is generally the protective one in the relationship. It was he who, they recollect, saved Estragon from drowning in the Rhône many years before, and he who, in one of the tenderest moments in the play, wraps his coat over the shoulders of the sleeping Estragon before walking up and down swinging his arms to keep warm. There are few enough consolations in a play about the futility of hope and desire, but these small moments of kindness, frail and unavailing though they may be, reveal shards of fellow-feeling and human decency that are at some level redemptive.

But if the play recognises moments of kindness brought on by adversity, it also highlights the brutality and domination that so often characterises human relations. Most obviously this occurs in Pozzo's treatment of Lucky, but even from Vladimir and Estragon the impulse to exploit emerges on occasion. When Pozzo reappears in Act II, Vladimir is intrigued to see his incapacity: 'You mean we have him at our mercy?' (78). The master–slave opposition between Pozzo and Lucky, the material exploitation of the latter by the former, is so elaborate that one is tempted to see it as a parody of the sort of social domination of which political radicals and reformers might complain. So exaggerated is Pozzo's maltreatment of Lucky, so hyperbolically and gratuitously brutal, that the niceties, formality and scrupulousness of his conversation with the two tramps seems comically anomalous. For all the refinement he shows to them—and in contrast to the utter inhumanity he shows to the hapless slave—he is aware of the difference in his own social rank and that of the two tramps: 'Yes, gentlemen, I cannot go for long without the society of my likes (he puts on his glasses and looks at the two likes) even when the likeness is an imperfect one' (21). The two vagrants also recognise social superiority when they see it. Pozzo is addressed as 'Sir', while Lucky only merits the less deferential 'Mister'. Such locutions as 'Oh I say!' or 'My good man' identify Pozzo as well-to-do English or, possibly, Anglo-Irish. Another facet of the power dynamic worthy of note here is that Lucky, while clearly standing in as an oppressed servant or slave, may also be the artist and intellectual figure. In the relationship of Pozzo and Lucky can be discerned a shadow of class relations between the land-owners or the wealthy and those that provide them with intellectual and aesthetic diversions: 'But for him all my thoughts, all my feelings, would have been of common things (*Pause. With extraordinary vehemence.*) Professional worries! (*Calmer*) Beauty, grace, truth of the first water, I knew they were all beyond me. So I took a knook'. (33)

Pozzo remarks at one point that he could have been in Lucky's shoes, and vice versa, 'If chance had not willed otherwise' (31). It is a telling use of this cliché. How can chance 'will' something? Of its nature, chance is will-less, and inanimate, outside the operations of even a blind determinism. If something happens by accident or chance, then an act of will has nothing to do with it. But *Waiting for Godot* is a play which, from the beginning, seeks to probe the 'why' of suffering. Or, perhaps more accurately, seeks to dramatise the condition of not knowing the answer to this question. It begins, after all, by asking why one of the thieves was saved but not the other. On what basis was the selection made? At the end of Act I, we discover that Godot beats one of the boys but not his brother, but for what reason? The boy does not know. The refrain within Lucky's speech, a parody of academic or philosophical attempts to understand the source of human suffering, is that human beings suffer 'for reasons unknown'. Here is another echo of the non-arrival of Godot. Vladimir does not receive an answer to his initial questions about the crucifixion. The mystery remains unsolved.

It is not enough simply to declare that Beckett's characters are 'innocent' sufferers. The problem is rather that their crime, the source of their guilt, is elusive. Punishment and damnation are dished out for seemingly inscrutable reasons. In Western culture the ultimate source of guilt, the primal transgression, is Original Sin. This is the stain with which, in the Judeo-Christian tradition, each person is born. *Waiting for Godot*, as we have seen, playfully alludes to this Edenic source but simultaneously deflates it. Early in the play, the pair consider what it is they should repent:

> VLADIMIR: Suppose we repented.
> ESTRAGON: Repented what?
> VLADIMIR: Oh ... (*He reflects.*) We wouldn't have to go into
>   the details.
> ESTRAGON: Our being born?
> (*Vladimir breaks into hearty laugh which he immediately stifles, his*
>   *hand pressed to his pubis, his face contorted.*) (11)

Years before, in *Proust*, Beckett has made another allusion to the sin of birth as part of a definition of tragedy:

> Tragedy is not concerned with human justice. Tragedy is the statement of an expiation, but not the miserable expiation of a codified breach of local arrangement, organized by the knaves for the fools. The tragic figure represents the expiation of the original sin, of the original and eternal sin ... of having been born. (67)

This excerpt is full of philosophical confidence to the point of pomposity: true tragedy is original and eternal and not at all concerned with 'local' issues such as justice or history. This disdain for politically motivated art in Beckett's early critical work would seem to strengthen the hand of those commentators who read *Waiting for Godot* as about a universal human condition. However, there are important differences between the notion of birth as sin in *Proust* and its recurrence in *Waiting for Godot*. In the later instance the assertion that original sin ought to be 'expiated' (how the expiation is effected is not explained in *Proust*, though the implication is that it has something to do with the catharsis of tragedy) has become a joke. The grandiosity of the aspiration is immediately undercut first by Vladimir's guffaw and then by his attempt, prompted by his painful urinary complaint, to stifle it. Once again the 'big idea', that might give us an interpretative hook on the play, is punctured as soon as uttered.

    There is little uncertainty about the tone of Proust which, as the disdain for the merely 'local' above attests, assumes a universal validity for its pessimistic pronouncements. 'Life' itself, marred as it is by destructive time and insatiable desire, is about boredom, habit and suffering. Blaming the debased condition of humanity on any political or social arrangements would be equivalent, to borrow a phrase of Vladimir's, to blaming on the boots the faults of the feet. From the earliest critical reception of *Waiting for Godot*, many commentators claimed that it had something fundamental to say about what it means to be human. In other words, the play does not simply have to do with particular people at a particular moment in history—it says something about the 'human condition' as a whole, outside history or politics, or any particular social situation.

The seeming withdrawal of *Waiting for Godot* from a world of specifics gives succour to this ahistorical view. The play is so bare and shorn of recognisable geographical reference that one might be tempted to read this as a sort of an archetypal space that can stand in for everywhere or anytime. The sparseness of the setting and the simplicity of the narrative suggest the play might be dealing with elemental truths. Admittedly there are a few scant references to particular places—to the Eiffel Tower, or to the River Rhône—which betray the original French in which the play was written. Lucky's reference to the 'skull in Connemara' gestures towards Beckett's Irish roots (though this is 'Normandie' in the original French version). Similarly Estragon asks Pozzo for ten francs. But at the same time there is a careful rootlessness in the staging and presentation. If Estragon's name has a French quality (it means tarragon), Vladimir's sounds more Russian. Pozzo's name sounds like a clown's and Lucky's like a household pet. In terms of their dialect, the two tramps speak English with an Irish cadence. So the national cues come from the various different parts of Europe with which Beckett was familiar. It leaves a plurality of sourcing that encourages the notion that this is everyplace. Vladimir ponders on Pozzo's call for assistance when he is prostrate in Act II: 'To all mankind they were addressed, those cries for help still ringing in our ears! But at this place, at this moment of time, all mankind is us, whether we like it or not' (79). A little later, Estragon remarks of Pozzo, 'He's all humanity' (83), just after the latter has answered to both the names Abel and Cain. We might remember that in the first act, Estragon has claimed his name is 'Adam', and of course one of the echoes of the lone tree on-stage is to the Garden of Eden. This association with the mythic origin of humankind allows the play to resonate, once more, with the elemental, the original and ultimately the universal. The answer, then, as to the representative status of the characters on stage is given by Estragon:

> VLADIMIR: We have kept our appointment, and that's an end
> to that. We are not saints, but we have kept our appointment.
> How many people can boast as much?
> ESTRAGON: Billions. (80)

Lines like this are further encouragement to read the play as a sort of an allegory of the human condition.

'The key word in my plays', Beckett told Tom Driver, 'is "perhaps".' It is paradoxical that a play with such an investment in the withholding of certainty, in the processes of confusion and bewilderment, would make such grandiose claims as to how things are. But, as ever, if this universal reading is suggested, it is like the idea of Godot as God, only one of many interpretative possibilities, all of which contribute to the overall aesthetic effect. The Edenic allusion is often so flagrant here that it teeters into irony, undoing through comic exaggeration any symbolic meaning it might hold. Moreover, how can we trust Estragon? His assertion that 'billions' keep their appointment is contradicted by his ignorance in almost all other facets. He cannot even remember what happened the previous day, so why should we take uncritically his assertions of catholicity? He is less reflective and intellectual than Vladimir and is mostly motivated by his next carrot or chicken bone. Vladimir thinks about the Bible, whereas Gogo simply admires the illustrations of the Holy Land. It is telling that the references to Eden come from the unreflective Gogo, rather than the cerebral and contemplative Vladimir. From this source, the allusions to the mythic origins of humanity are no sooner uttered than ridiculed.

The play is not translatable to a series of philosophical formulae nor, simply, to a pessimistic view of the human condition. Just as Beckett was uncomfortable with the label of 'Theatre of the Absurd', he disowned the idea that he had a systematically negative view of life, or any sort of synoptic overview from which judgement could be made:

> If pessimism is a judgement to the effect that ill outweighs good, then I can't be taxed with same, having no desire or competence to judge. I happen simply to have come across more of the one than the other.

There is too much uncertainty in his work, too much doubt and bewilderment, for clear interpretations to provide pat certainty. This is a play in which Godot does not arrive. Beckett renounced the abstract philosophical pronouncements of his younger self and, as we see from Lucky's 'think', came to regard academic philosophy and theology with scepticism. One suspects that Beckett was frustrated that the passages on time and habit in the play have been continually used as interpretative hooks. He felt, significantly, that 'the early success of *Waiting for Godot* was based on a fundamental misunderstanding, critics and public alike insisted on interpreting in allegorical or symbolic terms a play which was striving all the time to avoid definition'. *Waiting for Godot* is all about this avoidance of definition. Like Vladimir and Estragon, the audience and critics of the play are attendant on a meeting that is continually deferred.

Chronology

1906   Born Good Friday, April 13, at Foxrock, near Dublin, second son of William and Mary Beckett, middle-class Irish Protestants. Beckett claimed to have a vivid memory of his fetal existence. "It was an existence where no voice, no possible movement could free me from the agony and darkness I was subjected to." (Quoted in Cohn, *Back to Beckett*, vii)

1911   Attends kindergarten; said of his childhood: "You might say I had a happy childhood . . . although I had little talent for happiness. My parents did everything that could make a child happy. But I was often lonely." (Cohn, vii)

1912   Attends school in Dublin; begins to study piano and French.

1920   Attends Portora Royal School, Northern Enniskillen; plays cricket, rugby, tennis; also participates in swimming and boxing. Begins to write stories and poems; some are published in the school newspaper.

1923   Attends Trinity College in Dublin.

1928   Begins two-year fellowship in Paris; begins friendship with James Joyce; begins study of Descartes.

1929   Early writings in *Transition*.

1930   *Whoroscope* wins competition for best poem on the topic of "time."

1931	*Proust* published.
1932	Writes *Dream of Fair to Middling Women*; never published.
1933	Death of Beckett's father.
1934	*More Pricks Than Kicks.*
1936	Visits museums in Germany; expresses dismay about Nazi oppression of Jewish intellectuals.
1937	Returns to Paris; begins writing poems in French for first time. In November returns to Dublin as a witness in an anti-Semitic defamation trial.
1938	On a Paris street, Beckett sustains a serious stab wound in the chest by a stranger; Joyce writes to his son: "Beckett has had a lucky escape" (Cohn, x); *Murphy* published.
1940	Flees Paris with approach of Nazis. Later in year joins a Resistance network: "I couldn't stand with my arms folded" (Cohn, x). Later returns to Paris.
1942	Escapes hours before Nazis arrive to search his apartment.
1945	Serves as interpreter and storekeeper in a Red Cross field hospital in France.
1946	Begins five years of writing in French.
1950	Returns to Ireland in time to be with his dying mother.
1951	*Molloy* published.
1952	*Waiting for Godot* published.
1953	Premiere of *En attendant Godot* in Paris; *Watt, Malone Dies,* and *The Unnamable* published.
1955	*Waiting for Godot* opens in London.
1956	*Waiting for Godot* opens in Miami for first American performance.
1958	In February, the English Lord Chancellor banned production of *Endgame* in London because the Deity was called a bastard; ban lifted in November.
1959	Receives an honorary doctorate from Trinity College.
1961	*Comment c'est* published; shares International Publisher's Prize with Jorge Luis Borges.
1962	Marries Suzanne Dumesnil on March 25.
1964	Visits New York City to take part in producing his *Film*.
1969	Awarded the Nobel Prize in Literature while on vacation in Tunisia.
1972	*The Lost Ones.*

1973	*Not I.*
1976	*Ends and Odds; Fizzles; All Strange Away.*
1977	*... but the clouds ...*
1978	*Mirlitonnades* (35 short poems).
1980	*Company; One Evening.*
1981	*Ill Seen Ill Said; Rockaby.*
1983	*Catastrophe.*
1986	Diagnosed with emphysema; beginning of period of declining health.
1989	Dies in a Paris hospital, December 22; Suzanne died a half year earlier; buried next to her in the cemetery at Montparnasse on December 26.

Contributors

HAROLD BLOOM is Sterling Professor of the Humanities at Yale University. He is the author of 30 books, including *Shelley's Mythmaking, The Visionary Company, Blake's Apocalypse, Yeats, A Map of Misreading, Kabbalah and Criticism, Agon: Toward a Theory of Revisionism, The American Religion, The Western Canon,* and *Omens of Millennium: The Gnosis of Angels, Dreams, and Resurrection. The Anxiety of Influence* sets forth Professor Bloom's provocative theory of the literary relationships between the great writers and their predecessors. His most recent books include *Shakespeare: The Invention of the Human,* a 1998 National Book Award finalist, *How to Read and Why, Genius: A Mosaic of One Hundred Exemplary Creative Minds, Hamlet: Poem Unlimited, Where Shall Wisdom Be Found?,* and *Jesus and Yahweh: The Names Divine.* In 1999, Professor Bloom received the prestigious American Academy of Arts and Letters Gold Medal for Criticism. He has also received the International Prize of Catalonia, the Alfonso Reyes Prize of Mexico, and the Hans Christian Andersen Bicentennial Prize of Denmark.

RICHARD SCHECHNER originally published his work on Beckett in *Modern Drama* (1966).

WALTER ASMUS was a theater director in Germany and was Beckett's assistant in several Schiller-Theater productions.

MARTIN ESSLIN was professor of drama at Stanford University. He has also written *Brecht: A Choice of Evils; Pinter, the Playwright;* and *Mediations: Essays on Brecht, Beckett, and the Media.*

KATHERINE H. BURKMAN has also written on Harold Pinter's *The Homecoming* in *Harold Pinter: Critical Approaches* (1986).

NORMAND BERLIN has also written *The Secret Cause: A Discussion of Tragedy*. He was a member of the English department at the University of Massachusetts at Amherst.

MICHAEL WORTON is senior lecturer in French at University College in London. He co-edited *Intertextuality: Theories and Practice* (1990) and *Textuality and Sexuality: Reading Theories and Practices* (1993).

RUBY COHN was called "the doyenne of Beckett criticism" by *The Times Literary Supplement*. Besides her extensive work on Beckett she has written *Modern Shakespeare Offshoots*, *Dialogue in American Drama*, and *Currents in American Drama*. She teaches in the department of dramatic arts at the University of California at Davis.

CHRISTOPHER DEVENNEY teaches in the English department at Haverford College.

LOIS GORDON is the author of a biography of Beckett, *The World of Samuel Beckett* (1996).

GERRY DUKES lectures in English at the University of Limerick. He also published *Illustrated Lives: Samuel Beckett* (2001).

RÓNÁN MCDONALD is lecturer in English at the University of Reading and director of the Beckett International Foundation.

Bibliography

Brater, Enoch, ed. *Beckett at 80/Beckett in Context*. New York: Oxford University Press, 1986.

Burkman, Katherine H. *The Arrival of Godot*. Cranbury, NJ, London, and Ontario: Associated University Presses, 1986.

Calder, John. *The Philosophy of Samuel Beckett*. London: Calder Publications UK Ltd, 2001.

Cohn, Ruby. *A Beckett Canon*. Ann Arbor: University of Michigan Press, 2001.

———. *Back to Beckett*. Princeton: Princeton University Press, 1973.

———, ed. *Casebook on Waiting for Godot*. New York: Grove Press, 1967.

Connor, Steven. *Samuel Beckett: Repetition, Theory and Text*. Oxford: Basil Blackwell Ltd., 1988.

Essif, Les. *Empty Figure on an Empty Stage: The Theatre of Samuel Beckett and His Generation*. Bloomington and Indianapolis: Indiana University Press, 2001.

Esslin, Martin. *The Theatre of the Absurd*, third edition. Harmondsworth, Middlesex, England: Penguin Books Ltd., 1980.

———, ed. *Samuel Beckett: A Collection of Critical Essays*. Englewood Cliffs, NJ: Prentice-Hall, Inc., 1965.

Gontarski, S.E., ed. *On Beckett: Essays and Criticism*. New York: Grove Press, 1986.

Gordon, Lois. *Reading "Godot."* New Haven and London: Yale University Press, 2002.

Graver, Lawrence and Raymond Federman, eds. *Samuel Beckett: The Critical Heritage*. London, Henley and Boston: Routledge & Kegan Paul, 1979.

Hoffman, Frederick J. *Samuel Beckett: The Language of Self*. Carbondale: Southern Illinois University Press, 1962.

Kalb, Jonathan. *Beckett in Performance*. Cambridge: Cambridge University Press, 1989.

Kenner, Hugh. *A Reader's Guide to Samuel Beckett*. Syracuse, NY: Syracuse University Press, 1996.

Lyons, Charles R. *Samuel Beckett*. New York: Grove Press, 1983.

McDonald, Ronan. *The Cambridge Introduction to Samuel Beckett*. Cambridge: Cambridge University Press, 2006.

Murray, Christopher, ed. *Samuel Beckett: 100 Years*. Dublin: New Island Press, 2006.

Pilling, John, ed. *The Cambridge Companion to Beckett*. Cambridge: Cambridge University Press, 1994.

Sussman, Henry, and Christopher Devenney, eds. *Engagement and Indifference: Beckett and the Political*. Albany: State University of New York, 2001.

Acknowledgements

Richard Schechner, "There's Lots of Time in *Godot*," from *Casebook on Waiting for Godot*. © 1967 by Grove Press, Inc.

Walter D. Asmus, "Beckett Directs 'Godot,'" from *On Beckett: Essays and Criticism*. © 1986 by Grove Press, Inc.

Martin Esslin, "Introduction: The Absurdity of the Absurd," from *The Theatre of the Absurd*, copyright © 1961 by Martin Esslin. Used by permission of Doubleday, a division of Random House, Inc.

Katherine H. Burkman, "The Nonarrival of Godot: Initiation into the Sacred Void," from *The Arrival of Godot: Ritual Patterns in Modern Drama*, pp. 33-53. London and Toronto: Associated University Presses, 1986.

Normand Berlin, "The Tragic Pleasure of *Waiting for Godot*," from *Beckett at 80/Beckett in Context*. Used by permission of Oxford University Press, Inc.

Michael Worton, "*Waiting for Godot* and *Endgame:* Theatre as Text," from *The Cambridge Companion to Beckett*, © 1994. Reprinted with the permission of Cambridge University Press.

Ruby Cohn, "*En attendant Godot* (Waiting for Godot)," from *A Beckett Canon*. © 2001 by the University of Michigan.

Index